HIDDEN TREASURES REVEALED

TEACHING THE JEWISH ROOTS OF THE CHRISTIAN FAITH

PART 1

BY

JOHN F. PHELPS

© 2016 by Diann Ray Phelps. Published by haOr l'Olam Ministry. All Rights Reserved. No part of this book may be reproduced or transmitted in any form or by any means, electronic or mechanical, including photocopying, recording, or by any information storage or retrieval system, without permission in writing from the copyright holder. For information address Discipleship Ministry Team, Cumberland Presbyterian Church, 8207 Traditional Place, Cordova (Memphis), Tennessee, 38016-7414. Third Printing.

William Hallmark illustrations © 2016 (pages 35, 91, 105, & 121) are used by permission. If you are interested in William's artwork, contact him at (205) 541-2067.

Ethan A. McCoy photography © 2016 (cover, page 47) are used by permission. If you are interested in contacting Ethan, his number is 270-922-8935.

Compiled by Diann Ray Phelps
Edited by Maryanne L. Phelps

ha Or l' Olam Ministry
4743 Happy Hollow Rd.
Hawesville, KY 42348

Phone: 270-927-9835
haOr.lOlam@yahoo.com
www.haorlolamMinistry.org

ISBN 10: 194592006
ISBN 13: 978-1945929007

TABLE OF CONTENTS

FOREWORDS V
ACKNOWLEDGEMENTS VIII
PREFACE X
INTRODUCTION XV

CHAPTER ONE: BEGINNING THE JOURNEY
WHY STUDY JEWISH ROOTS 1
RECOGNIZING BIASES 7

CHAPTER TWO: FIRST DIG SITE
A DIFFERENT WAY OF THINKING 9
LANGUAGES JESUS SPOKE 12
THE LANGUAGE OF THE GOSPELS 18

CHAPTER THREE: FIRST TREASURES REVEALED
JEWISH EXPECTATIONS 21
MESSIANIC SIGNS 25
JESUS AS A BOY 34
HIS MESSIANIC CLAIM 38

CHAPTER FOUR: NUGGETS OF TRUTH
JESUS' BAPTISM 42
IDIOMS 46
FULFILLING THE LAW 53
BINDING AND LOOSING 57
CIRCUMLOCUTION 64

CHAPTER FIVE: TOOLS THAT JESUS USED
PARABLES 70
PARABLES: THE PRODIGAL SON 74
LIGHT AND HEAVY 77
MEASURE FOR MEASURE 82
REMEZ 84

CHAPTER SIX: JESUS' FAVORITE TOOL
NATHANAEL 89

    JESUS IN NAZARETH 93
    JOHN'S EXPECTATION 95
    SON OF MAN 97

CHAPTER SEVEN: WHAT CHANGED
    MESSIANIC CLAIM BECAME BOLDER 102
    THE TRIUMPHANT ENTRY 105
    OVERTURNING THE TABLES 107
    WHO KILLED JESUS 108
    TWO MESSIAHS 116
    ON THE THIRD DAY 119

RESOURCES
    JOHN'S RECOMMENDATIONS 123
    SUGGESTED BIBLIOGRAPHY 128
    INDEX OF TERMS 130

FOREWORDS

Few people who had the pleasure of meeting John Phelps would ever forget him! His effervescent personality, boundless energy, broad smile and resonant bass voice were captivating. Johnny and I met as incoming college freshmen and immediately formed a lasting friendship. We had so much in common: both were sons of pastors, both enthralled with music and drama, both involved in intramural sports, both dedicated students, and both preparing for ministry one day. We formed a folk duo, playing guitars and singing the songs of the early 'sixties. Though after college our times together were too infrequent, when our paths did cross, it was as if we'd never been apart. Over the years my respect for him only grew, as I knew of his pastoral work, his ministry in education, and particularly his work with Jewish Roots studies -- though I did not have the opportunity to learn from him in this regard.

Now that has changed. With the publication of *Hidden Treasures Revealed*, I feel I've been able to sit in a seminar with him, listening to his passionate and insightful probing of Scripture, and inspired by his exhaustive research into the languages and customs of the Jewish world of which Jesus Christ was a part. Thanks to the arduous work Diann has done in preserving his notes and recorded teaching sessions, these lessons are now in a format that can be used through the generations. Though these pages reflect a depth of keen scholarship, they read as if John is simply talking with his friends about matters of great urgency from Scripture in disarmingly down-to-earth ways.

There are many "treasures" in this book, not the least of which is a glimpse into the Spirit-filled mind and heart of that Godly man, John Phelps.

George R. Estes ~ (B.A.-Bethel U.; M.Div. - Memphis Theological Seminary; D. Min. - Austin Presbyterian Theological Seminary); Cumberland Presbyterian pastor, denominational missions staff leader and adjunct seminary professor.

God blessed John Phelps with one of the keenest minds I have witnessed. His knowledge of the New Testament and Judaism brought glory to God, even before John realized his passion for the relationship between the two. I studied the Old Testament with John at Vanderbilt University. Dr. Herbert May, our professor, immediately recognized John's unique gift to see the critical relationship between Judaism and Christianity. However, John's thoughts and writing didn't reach their potential until his mind and heart came under the influence and control of Almighty God, through a personal conversion experience midway through his life. His explanations of the treasures in Jewish writing open the doors for a clearer interpretation of the teachings of the New Testament and the daily practice of personal faith in Jesus Christ. This book will grab and hold your attention. I highly recommend it!

Dr. Robert Watkins ~ (B.S. - Bethel U; M. Div., Dr. of Ministry - Vanderbilt U.); missionary to Colombia, SA; Director of Global Mission for the Cumberland Presbyterian Denomination and has authored several books.

I had the honor and privilege of meeting John Phelps on a couple of occasions when he was a guest teacher/preacher at my home church, First United Methodist Church, in Columbia, MS. John approached Jesus' words and actions in a way I had never heard. As a teacher of the Men's Bible Class for 11 years, I was already intrigued with the history and customs of the Bible. Only after listening to John's teachings, both in person and on CD, did I realize I was only scratching the surface of what Jesus is saying to us as Christians. John's teachings make the words and actions of Jesus come alive. He was able to express the teachings and sayings of Jesus and the Jewish customs associated with Jesus' teachings in such a way that you yearn to learn more. John truly got to the essence of what Jesus was really saying when He spoke. I am thrilled to know that some of John's teachings are now being compiled into this book. My words cannot adequately convey the excitement that I have over the release of this book. Having his teachings in written word for constant discernment and reflection can only strengthen one's faith in our LORD and Savior, Jesus Christ.

Hal Kittrell ~ B.A. - U. MS; Juris D.- U. MS Law; District Attorney -15th Circuit Court District of MS; Fellow MS Bar Foundation; President - MS Prosecutors Assoc.

In a culture where folks no longer understand the value of absolute truth, this work is extremely refreshing. In Hidden Treasures Revealed, Author John Phelps along with his beloved wife, Diann share timeless eternal truths. These eternal truths are like nuggets of gold waiting to be discovered. In any archaeological dig, one never knows what treasure lies just beneath the next layer of earth. These ancient nuggets will transform the way one interprets the Word of God and the way that so many see and understand Jesus Christ. Dig in and allow yourself the luxury of meditating upon these truths that are far more valuable than jewels.

Thank you, John and Diann, for your lifetime of hard work and sharing the discoveries of your labor with us.

Rev. Dr. Jacqueline DeBerry ~ B.S. - Bethel U; M. Div., D. Min. – Memphis Theological Seminary; BCI; BCPC: pastor, teacher, counselor, and chaplain.

ACKNOWLEDGEMENTS

First and foremost, I want to thank the LORD for His guidance and direction as I attempted a nearly impossible task for me. You see, I am dyslexic, and thus I am not a reader. This project has definitely stretched me way past my comfort zone. Also, I so appreciate John for his great love of the LORD, his zeal to be an essential part of maturing the Bride, and for leaving behind a well-spring of materials. He began taping his messages in 1986, at my mother's encouragement. When we began *'haOr l'Olam Ministry,'* he continued taping. It would truly take me another lifetime to transform all of his teachings and sermons into written form.

Second, I want to thank William Hallmark and Ethan McCoy for their art work and photography in this book. William's sketches add so much to the book. He is a renowned Christian Artist and a friend. I truly appreciate him taking the time to be a part of this project. Ethan, my grandson-in-law, captured my vision for the cover page and the photo on page 49. I also want to thank my grandson, Joshua Wilborn, for his patience while being photographed for the cover page.

I want to thank our daughter-in-law, Maryanne Phelps, for her editing skills and patience. I know it has not been easy with the long-distance communications and the many times I changed the order of things. I would also like to thank our son, John B. Phelps, for his amazing computer assistance in all of those tough spots.

I want to thank all those that were my go-to sources when I was stuck: David Bivin and Clif Payne are both Jewish Roots scholars and were able to help me find references to several of John's quotes; our daughter,

Kim Wilborn, for the many times she looked up scriptures for me, and for believing in me through this arduous project; and Phillip Layne for his help in the area of historical facts, and being a great support.

I also want to thank all those that took the time to write forewords for this book. I truly appreciate their kind words and endorsements.

Last but not least, I want to thank Beth El Shaddai for their support of our ministry, both through prayer and financially for so many years. I also want to thank all those that opened their pulpits and gave John the opportunity to share his message, and for those that have donated to the ministry.

~ *Diann Ray Phelps*

PREFACE

This book is made up of the teachings of Rev. John F. Phelps. John lost his battle to cancer July 19, 2008. The books the LORD had instructed John to write are being compiled from his notes and recorded teachings. I felt myself inadequate for such a task, so I handed the project over to others that knew and loved John, but after many attempts, it became clear that I was the one that God had assigned this task. It is impossible to capture the zeal with which John delivered his teachings, but hopefully the content will be a blessing to you.

I would like to share John's story, and in that, hopefully, you will see why the Jewish Roots study was so important to him. John gave his heart to the LORD at the age of 8, and felt a call to ministry at the age of 13. He attended Bethel College to prepare for that calling. John and I met his sophomore year, actually my first day on campus. We were married at the end of his junior year. He graduated Summa Cum Laude from Bethel, and received a full scholarship to Vanderbilt University where he went on to graduate the top of his class there, receiving the Founders Medal. Vanderbilt offered him a full scholarship to continue for his Doctorate with a teaching position guaranteed, but he declined.

John had begun to question his faith while at Bethel, and under the teaching of some of the professors in Seminary, he lost his faith. He was a third-generation Cumberland Presbyterian minister, but unlike his father and grandfather, he preached for 15 years not believing the Bible to be true. He believed there were truths in it and it was his job to pick and choose. John saw God as the watchmaker that had set everything in motion and left the rest up to us. He did not believe in the virgin birth, that Jesus was the son of God, life after death, or miracles. His New Testament professor, Robert Funk, later founded the Jesus Seminar in California, where scholars would gather and vote on what they felt were actually Jesus' words, and discarded all but one statement in the gospel of John.

After graduation, John taught school, preached at my home church, was a volunteer fireman, volunteer EMT, and was involved in many giving activities. When John preached the truth of God's word, people's lives were changed; three young men were called to the ministry under his preaching. Even though John's life was out of order, God's word will not return void.

John was a good man. In 1985, this God that didn't get involved in our lives, did. In his own words, *"God started messing with me."* First, my Mom had *Guidepost* sent to our home. He picked up the April '85 issue and read the testimony of Barbara Cummiskey. She had gone from an active 15-year-old gymnast in 1965, to having major physical problems. She was later diagnosed with MS, and by 1978, she was in a wheelchair, and the Doctors could do nothing. Then in 1981, she heard *"My child, get up and walk."* She knew His voice, so she stood and walked, and all physical control and ability was restored to her. After reading this, John yelled out, *"Diann, miracles are real!"* Her testimony had stretched his understanding of God. That same year, he was given a book on Life After Death experiences. He read it, and through it began to believe that there is something after this life. God was dealing with him personally and this made him very angry. That summer, he had agreed to be the evangelist for two churches in our Presbytery for a minister friend, Robert Milam. He became angry as the time approached for agreeing to do it, but he kept his word. He was in the middle of the first revival at the Short Creek C. P. Church, and God intervened in his life.

From John's recorded testimony:

I had never felt so empty. I sat down to prepare my sermon and as I began to write, I began to weep. I wept while I wrote 8 pages. I know the first few lines by heart. **"You don't know who you're dealing with. You are dealing with a God that is so great, you cannot begin to imagine His power. You are dealing with a God that is so vast that your imagination cannot grasp the scope of His magnitude. You are dealing with a God that is so wise,"** *(and I was a Philosophy major),* **"that all men's wisdom and philosophy pales in comparison."** *And then He went on, superlative after superlative until it got to the bottom line, and on that bottom line, on that first page, it broke my heart and changed my life. It said,* **"But He is a God that loves you so much that He wants you to call Him Father."** *I said, "I give up. I'm yours. Wherever you want me to go." In that instant, for the first time, I had accepted Him as* LORD *of my life, and surrendered to His* LORDSHIP, *and at that moment, everything changed. The burden was lifted; the peace was there. It was like I had been born afresh. I had accepted Jesus years before, but I had never let*

Him be LORD *of my life. I said, "I don't know You, I know about You, and I'm not smart enough to know what I need to know and what I don't, so You're going to have to teach me." The adventure began that day and has never ended. Within two weeks, I got a call to a church in Clinton, OK, within two months, my wife, two children and I, were packed up and moving* (John did not have his resume out looking for a church, and a church 800 miles away from home, family, and friends called him).

In 1987, while in Clinton, Oklahoma, John became involved in a Full Gospel group. He was doing the music one evening when Hemline Specter, founder of Rock of Israel Ministry, spoke to the group. After it was over, we stood outside for hours, and as John said, *"it began to stir that something was missing."* Then, when we moved to Birmingham, AL, we became involved with World Wide Jewish Missions, and that led us to Beth El Shaddai, where John became their spiritual leader; he was pastoring a traditional church at the same time. During our time at Beth El Shaddai, John became close friends with Clif Payne. Clif introduced him to the teachings of the Jewish School of Synoptic Studies. The more John learned, the more these studies answered the questions that he had had in seminary. He discovered that "Yes, Jesus was the Messiah, the Son of God, and He knew He was."

John and I felt the call to travel and teach the Jewish Roots of the Christian faith. John felt the LORD's leading in naming the ministry *"haOr l'Olam,"* which is Hebrew for "The Light of the World," Matthew 5:14.

We began the second phase of our wonderful adventure in September of 1997, going wherever the LORD opened doors. John once described our adventure with the LORD as "going down white water rapids in a boat without an oar. It is so very exciting and scary at the same time." A Jewish scholar told him, he had just described "*the fear of the LORD.*" It was an awesome adventure, and I praise the LORD for allowing us to be a part of His ministry. As you delve into this study, I pray that it will excite you, and increase your love for Yeshua (Jesus), our Messiah (Christ) as it did for us, as we discovered and shared these truths. I hope you can see John's zeal for the nuggets of truth he discovered, and understand why this was so very important to John.

~ *Diann Ray Phelps*

INTRODUCTION

This is a direct quote from John before beginning the Jewish Roots study and it is a word to you as well:

"I want you to gain three things from these teachings:

Number one, I want you to gain an appreciation that there is more in the Scripture than you have seen before, and that there are rich treasures to be found once we learn when and where and how to dig.

Number two, I want you to become familiar with resources that you can turn to, places you can go for information, for background studies, to find what you need when you need it.

None of us carry all of the information in ourselves and no one source has all the answers. So, number one is an appreciation that there is more in the text than we have seen. Number two is knowing where to look to begin to open up those doors.

*Number three, this is the most important one of all, to let the text impact us so suddenly we say: "You mean this is what God expects of me, and this is what I need to do?" In other words, if this teaching does not somehow show us how God wants us to respond to Him, then we haven't really grown. If all we have gained is information and knowledge, I have failed to reach my goal for you and this teaching. I want ultimately for these teachings to result in you being either a better student of the Bible, or **more deeply in love with Jesus** than ever before, or a **better witness** of your faith than ever before.*

Whether it is a formal setting or private setting, my goal is for you to be able to counter some of the lies of the enemy, for you to be able to have some information that can be shared with others and see them become excited about the word of God. It's more than trivia, it is something that impacts our lives. So these are the goals that we're shooting for."

In His Service,

John F. Phelps

John F. Phelps

CHAPTER ONE
BEGINNING THE JOURNEY

WHY STUDY JEWISH ROOTS

This quantitative process is important! There are many reasons for this study, but <u>the goal is to deepen our love for Jesus (Yeshua), our Messiah</u>, to deepen <u>our understanding, and broaden our knowledge of God's message</u>. The overall purpose is to make us more obedient and faithful, in our lives, to our LORD. This study should make us better witnesses of God's truth! There is a saying: 'Greeks read to understand, while Jews read to revere and obey.' I desire for the Scriptures to come alive for you. It is the 'Truth' that we are seeking to gain for our lives!

We will look at three basic reasons:

First: There have been, and continue to be, some misrepresentations of the Scripture. At times, the Church has taken teachings of Paul or teachings of Jesus and have misapplied it, much to the damage of the Church! Peter even writes about this in 2nd Peter 3:15,16, *"our beloved brother Paul...has written to you...in which some things are hard to understand."* Peter goes on to say, *"Untaught and unstable people twist to their own destruction, as they do also the rest of the Scripture."* Did you catch that? Peter was saying that Paul's letters were being considered Scripture, long before the canonization of the New Testament. The main point here is that misunderstanding Scripture, <u>causes great destruction!</u> Women have been put into bondage by the misrepresentation of what Paul had to say! In 1st Corinthians 11:4,5, Paul said, *"every woman who prays or prophesies with her head uncovered, she dishonors her head..."* Women's hair was considered seductive. Even today, in some Middle-Eastern cultures, women still keep their head covered. It has been said that the prostitutes of that day were punished by having their heads shaved. It is believed that Paul was referring to the ordinance against the shaving of one's head.[1] Paul was saying, 'women, when you stand and speak the word of the LORD, do it in an appropriate way, cover your head so the men won't be tempted or distracted.' When women "Prophesy or Pray," Paul is saying that women have the right to speak in a public worship service. To prophesy was to speak a revealed word from God, through an individual! Prophecy can be concerning the past, the present, or the future, but it is a word from God to the people for now! God doesn't concern Himself with the gender of His vessels, but uses whomever He chooses to use. When we take Paul's words out of the culture of his day, we miss the point of what he was saying, thus people are put into bondage!

In 1st Timothy 2:12, Paul wrote, *"and do not permit women to teach or have authority over a man."* Paul had a good reason for saying that. The Pharisees had established schools in nearly every village for the boys. Their formal education in the Scripture began at the age of five, and continued until age twelve.[2] The teaching method was 'Scripture explains Scripture.' Since the women were not formally educated in the Scripture,

---
1. www.wikipedia.com, Shaving in Judaism.
2. Bivin, David, New Life on the Difficult Words of Jesus, pp. 4,5.

they could not teach. Timothy was speaking among the Jews in Lycaonia.[3] The Gentile women were often leaders in the pagan religions, and Paul did not want any of the pagan teachings contaminating the church. It was not acceptable to teach from one's own opinion. However, to prophesy was to speak a revealed word from God. Women that are educated in the Scriptures, have as much right to teach as men. To be a teacher, one must be a student of the Word! When we look beyond the surface, at the culture of the Jewish people of the First Century, we gain new insights! <u>We study the Jewish Roots to correct the misinterpretation that has been passed down for centuries.</u>

    Second: We need a deeper understanding of the teachings and of the events that are found in the New Testament. Even through the events, God is speaking to us about the purpose, the design, and the meaning! Through Jesus' life, God is teaching us! In the Gospel of John 1:1, he tells us, *"In the beginning was the Word, and the Word was with God, and the Word was God,"* and John 1:14, *"The Word became Flesh and dwelt among us,"* that was Yeshua, Jesus! If Jesus is the Word of God, when Jesus spoke, it was <u>God speaking</u>! He was teaching us what God meant, showing us what God is like through every part of His life. So, it is important to understand the events of Jesus' life, as well as His teachings. I want to know what God has to say, don't you?

    Third: Judaism is our Birth Mother. It is very important that you understand this. <u>We do not replace Israel in God's plan.</u> God's promises are yes and Amen! Paul says this very clearly in Romans 11, there were

---

3. Hayford, Jack, Nelson's New King James, General Edition, p. 1839.

certain natural branches that reject God's way and they are cut off; Paul tells us to *pray that they are reunited.* <u>We are grafted in</u>! We joined the faithful Jewish community in doing the work! The big question among the Jewish believers in the First Century was, "<u>Do we take this message to the Gentiles or not?</u>" Today, the big question is, "<u>Do we take this message to the Jews or not?</u>"

I want to interject a fact that you might find interesting. When grafting a fruit tree, the branch from another tree is bound to a branch of the host tree. This is not how an olive tree is grafted. A piece of a wild olive branch is grafted to the root of an olive tree! It draws its nourishment from the root, not from other branches! "We are <u>grafted into the root</u>." If we were grafted onto the branch, we would be dependent on the Jewish community for our nourishment. Instead, we draw our nourishment directly from the root and we are allowed to become our own tree, in our own right. We do not replace that tree; we are grafted into the foundation. We <u>stand alongside it</u>. On a trip to Israel, we visited the Garden of Gethsemane where we saw a tree that was over 2,000 years old. That's one thing about an olive tree, they are almost indestructible! As long as there is any life in the root, that little piece of root will grow a tree!

In Galatians 3:6-29, Paul tells us, we that are not ethnically Jewish are called *"Children of Abraham,"* not Children of Moses. Why? Moses represents the Law! Abraham was the <u>man of Faith</u>! Paul says in verse 29, *"If you are in Christ then you are Abraham's seed and heirs according to the promise."* Also in Galatians 3:7, *"Therefore know that only those who are of faith are sons of Abraham."* So, if we are of faith, we are an offspring of Abraham.

To understand many of our concepts, we need a

fundamental understanding of First Century Judaism. To understand *Atonement,* we need to go back to "The Day of Atonement," found in Leviticus 23:26-32. To understand why Jesus had to die, why that sacrifice was required, we have to go back to what was required to atone for a sin, how to be reconciled to God. God laid out an elaborate picture to help us understand fully what Jesus did! The way I like to explain it is: in the Old Testament, God sketches the picture as an artist would sketch. In the New Testament, He fills in the colors. It is the same picture, for He is the same God of the Old Testament and the New Testament. We cannot separate the Old Testament from the New Testament! Marcion separated the two in the Second Century. He was declared a heretic by the Church.[4] Some maintain this thinking to this day, discounting the validity of the Old Testament. Jesus came as an Orthodox Jewish man of the First Century. His scripture is our Old Testament!

An in-depth study can become all-consuming and captivating. It saddens me to say that I know of people that have become so captivated by the Jewish studies, they literally renounced Jesus as Messiah and converted to Judaism! God is not pleased with that! I love the way Paul put it, "If you're born a Jew, then stay a Jew. If you're not Jewish, stay that way." The Messianic movement allows a Jew to accept Yeshua as Messiah and retain his Jewishness. Our goal is to recognize the Jewish heritage of the Christian faith!

Christianity is <u>concept oriented</u>. Christianity depends on the application of principles in our lives within a variety of cultural concepts, so that the Chinese,

---

4. Moseley, Dr. Ron, *Yeshua,* pp. 34-36.

or the Spanish, or the Americans can celebrate the LORD in different ways, yet still be brothers and sisters in the LORD! <u>Christianity is not conditioned by culture</u>, it is designed to condition culture, and that is a significant difference between Christianity and other religions.

Most religions require their converts to adopt certain cultural principles to be a part of their belief system. In the letters of Paul, he referred to the concept of putting ourselves under a bondage of reinstituting certain practices. Some of these issues were whether or not to worship on *Sabbath,* which is Saturday, to keep *Kosher*, to wear fringes, or to worship with the head covered or uncovered. He stated, <u>we are Free in Christ!</u> God's message is Universal; it is not restricted by culture. We do not have to go back and adopt a cultural position to be faithful to God.

Is it wrong to celebrate the feasts, or to wear a *Tallit* (the Prayer Shawl), or to keep *Kosher*? No, if you feel God is leading you to do so, then do it, but don't feel that everyone else is supposed to follow; God gives specific instructions to individuals. A lady shared her story with me. God specifically told her that she could not wear jeans, but she never tried to impose that rule on anyone else. She knew why He had told her that, and that it was specific to her situation. If we try to direct other's lives, we can kill their joy.

The goal of this study is to better equip us to understand our Holy Scripture, so that we can give a better account of ourselves when we are called to do so, or when our faith is challenged. We need to be able to counter the world's response: "What you believe and what I believe are different. Your truth is no greater than my truth!" We need to have a solid base of fundamental principles so that we can effectively share what our faith says and why! We want to present God in a whole new way and hopefully open eyes to His Love. I've found over and over again that whenever the 'Jewish Roots' are presented, people have to come to grips with who Jesus is and what His position in their lives should be! Their zeal for the LORD increases!

RECOGNIZING BIASES

Did you ever wonder why Israel's name was changed to Palestine? Angered by the *Bar Kochba* revolt against the Romans in 135 AD, Emperor Hadrian found a way to punish the Israelites to this day. He took the ancient enemies of Israel, the Philistines, and Latinized the name to *Palestine* and applied it to the land of Israel, hoping to erase the name Israel from all memory. Thus, the term *Palestine*, as applied to the Holy Land of Israel, was invented by Emperor Hadrian, enemy of the Bible and the Jewish people. The original Philistines were not even Middle-Eastern; they were European people from the Adriatic Sea near Greece.[5]

The writings of Peter and others can be misleading, concerning their attitude toward the Jews. Peter was writing to the Jewish body that had accepted Jesus as their Messiah, so they knew that when he said, *"the Jews killed Jesus."* He was speaking of the corrupt High Priest and his followers. However, because of such statements in the New Testament, as years passed,

---

5. www.levitt.com, Zola Levitt Ministry Article, Palestine vs Israel.

strong anti-Jewish biases developed in the church and horrible things were done in the name of Christ. During the First Century, ninety-five percent of the church was Jewish, and the early church considered themselves Jewish. It tells us in Luke 24:52,53, after Jesus' ascension, His followers "...*returned to Jerusalem with great joy, and were continually in the temple praising and blessing God.*" Acts 3:1 says, "*Now Peter and John went up together to the temple at the hour of prayers.*" Over and over, Scripture tells us that the disciples and believers went to the temple. They, Paul or the disciples, did not think of themselves as starting a new religion. The number of Jewish believers in Yeshua by 70 AD has been greatly underestimated. Dr. Shmuel Safrai estimated that by 70 AD, there were over 50,000-80,000 believers in Jesus, in Jerusalem and the surrounding areas, not including the Galilee region.[6]

    A strong anti-Jewish attitude still exists in much of the Christian community to this day. That is why the *Jewish Roots* study is so very important. We seek to change errors, recognize the foundational principles of the Old Testament, and realize that God's promises to His people are still in effect.

---

6. www.youtube.com/watch?y=XKvP1mWO2Vg, Bivin, David. An explanation is given on the translation of Acts 21:20, that leads to this misconception.

CHAPTER TWO
FIRST DIG SITE

A DIFFERENT WAY OF THINKING

The study of the Jewish Roots of Christianity is about rediscovering the foundational principles that under-gird not only our New Testament, but the subsequent development of the Church. Shortly after the time of Jesus, within a few generations, the non-Jewish believers outnumbered the Jewish believers. As things changed, such as centers of population, and social and economic settings, more and more the Church became the product of Athens rather than of Jerusalem. We say 'Athens' rather than Rome because Athens actually is the center of Greek culture. The Romans copied the Greek patterns from the Athenians when they established their empire. The thinking patterns that most westerners possess is basically Greek thinking!

There is one way that Greeks think, and another way that Jewish scholars thought. Greeks think linear: A leads to B, which leads to C, which concludes with D. We get our logic, as well as our deductive reasoning, from the Greeks. We pride ourselves with being able to move logically from A to B to C to D.

Jewish thinking is association, not linear progression, not in a straight line. In Jewish thinking: A associates with J, which reminds them of L, which brings them to K, which leads them to D! It is not a logical step by step process, like the Greeks use. Often, women's thinking process follows this pattern. They arrive at their conclusion in a more roundabout way, and in a very Jewish Manner. My wife and I would often be having a discussion and she would suddenly, out of the clear blue, make a statement. I would say, "Whoa! Stop. Tell me how you got there." She would reply, "Well, this reminded me of that and made me think of this, so I said this." It was perfectly logical, given the style of thinking, given that it had structure. It was not the Greek pattern of logic; which men predominately tend to use. It is the process of thinking 'associative,' which can be very difficult for Greek thinkers.

This is part of the problem! Our Scripture was written by Jewish people and translated into Greek. In order to understand the Scriptures, we have to understand the Jewish mind, their way of thinking in the First Century! We have to understand the Jewish principles of value, and what they did not value, some of the things that we value highly, they did not value at all.

An example: Chronology, we like to record things in the order that they occur. Why is this important? The Jewish mind did not put a value on the chronological order of things. They put what was important first and how it associated with something else. This is often described as a 'Spider Web' or 'Net' form of thinking, where one point of intersection connects with several different points, and can then go in any of the 'associated' ways. As they moved through this pattern, everything interlocked with everything else and the result was a "Pattern of Thinking," which is often very foreign to us.

A perfect example of this kind of thinking is in the Book of Numbers, it begins: "*In the second month of the second year after God led the Children of Israel out of Egypt the* LORD *said to Moses....*" In chapter nine of the

Book of Numbers, it says, *"In the first month of the second year after God led the children of Israel out of Egypt the* LORD *said to Moses...."* Chapter nine actually occurs a month prior to chapter one! Why was it put there? Because in their minds, time wasn't important! They presented what was needed to be established first. It's a Semitic approach. That's why we shouldn't be disturbed if the account of David and Goliath, and David's playing for Saul seem to be in conflict with one another. Or that Saul doesn't recognize the boy that had been playing for him; those stories are most likely not in chronological order.

You see, that was the way Jewish people of Jesus' time thought. That is why Luke wrote in his Gospel: *"...it seems good to me...to write to you in an orderly account,"* meaning he is going to attempt to put it in a chronological order, because his audiences were much more Greek than Hebrew, and needed the chronological order. When we try to read the Scriptures with a Western mindset, it can be very difficult to understand what is being said. Usually, when we find a passage that we don't understand, we just skip over it. The whole purpose of studying the Jewish Roots of the Christian Faith is to try to find the underlying principles that will help us read and understand our Scriptures better. The goal of these teachings is to open our minds to the hidden truths in our Scriptures. In order to do that successfully, we need to step back, out of time, out of our own century, into the First Century! Why? Because there are a variety of influences that are not true about our society today that were true about their society then. Things that show how they expressed themselves, what they felt was important, and what they naturally assumed everyone else knew. This is a big one, 'what they assumed everyone knew.' I have heard comments like, "well, the New Testament doesn't condemn it." That was because everyone knew how God felt about certain subjects, and there was no need to discuss it. When we mention the American flag, we don't go into a description of what it looks like, because we all know!

We have to understand that the New Testament was not written by Greek thinkers. The New Testament was written by Jews, yes, Jews. Most were not scholars, they were either eyewitnesses that gave accounts of things they saw and heard, or Disciples of the eyewitnesses and wrote what had been shared with them. They wrote from the position of their responses to those situations in their culture. If we are to understand the New Testament, we have to understand Judaism. Not the Judaism of today, but Judaism of what is called 'The Second Temple Period.'

LANGUAGES JESUS SPOKE

One of the most important things that we have to understand is the language that Jesus ministered in. For years, we have been taught that Jesus spoke Aramaic. Aramaic is a variant Semitic language, similar to Hebrew. They have many shared words, but are different enough that we have to know each language to be able to fully converse. The proof is in 2nd Kings 18:26, in the story of Rabshakeh who was speaking to the leaders in Hebrew. I am going to paraphrase what occurred: the leaders of Jerusalem said, 'Don't speak in Hebrew, speak in Aramaic, we understand it.'

Rabshakeh replied 'No, we want to communicate in your language so that everyone on the city walls listening, will know exactly what will happen if you follow your plan, and don't surrender.' Now, if Aramaic and Hebrew were exactly the same language, like some have tried to suggest, or similar enough to understand, then this whole story makes no sense! It only makes sense when we understand that Aramaic, which developed in the Babylonian region, was a variant language, kindred to Hebrew; it would be like Portuguese and Spanish. There are enough similarities between the two that one could catch certain words, but really can't converse fully, unless they know the individual languages. Hebrew and Aramaic are variants of the same language. At the time of Jesus (*Yeshua*), both languages were used. After the Babylonian captivity, Aramaic became the language of Israel until the time of the Maccabees. With the Maccabees, Hebrew started coming back as the spoken and written language of the land.[7]

Then, what language did Jesus speak? I feel, without a doubt, that I can establish the three languages that Jesus spoke. We have scripture that shows us that Jesus spoke in the three languages of that time and area: Aramaic, which was still the language of Samaria and the countryside; Hebrew, which had come back as a language; and of course, Greek. Why Greek? That was the language of the Roman Empire. It seems odd that Greek would be the spoken language because Latin was the language of Rome, but Latin was basically a formal written language. It was a very difficult language to

---

7. www.jewishencyclopedia.com, Temple, The Second.

speak. Because of Alexander the Great, the Romans simply adopted Greek, thus the Greek language had spread all over the known world.[8] Virtually all business dealings took place in the Greek language.

How do we know what language Jesus spoke? Let's see what Scripture tells us. We know that Jesus spoke to the people from the countryside and from Samaria, so He would have been using Aramaic. If, as I was taught, the only language that Jesus spoke was Aramaic, then why would certain terms be left in the Aramaic language in the text? When there was an Aramaic word used, they would insert it into the text, rather than translate it, as we might do with, say a French word. We now know that the original text was not written in Aramaic, it was written in Hebrew. Jesus' name in Hebrew was *Yeshua*, which means Salvation. It was the fifth most common name of His day.

Hebrew had once again become the language of Israel. It was the language of the politicians and of commerce, as well as the Rabbis. It was the written and spoken language of Jerusalem and Judea. How do we know? We know because texts written in Hebrew have been found, such as bills of sale. The best example would be the *Dead Sea Scrolls*, written by the *Essenes*. The *Essenes'* writings were all in Hebrew; their instruction, their Book of Discipline, and their reflections on the teachings on righteousness. These writings were contemporary to the time of Jesus! Many of these books that have been found are written in what is called *Mishnaic* Hebrew. That was the Hebrew that had been developed during the time of the *Mishnah*. The Mishnah

---

8. www.ancient.eu, Alexander the Great.

recorded the sayings of the sages that taught from approximately 550 BC to 200 AD. It is a collection of the Oral Law, the Rabbinic rulings on the Law.[9]

Josephus was a well-respected Jewish writer of the First Century. He began his writings as a captured general, then went on to become well respected in Rome. Even though he was a First Century Jew, he did not compose in Hebrew. His writings were done for the Romans, so it was in the language of his audience.

How do we know Jesus spoke Greek? Remember, He spoke with the Centurion, the Syro-phoenician woman, and others. They would not have been speaking Hebrew or Aramaic. They would have communicated in Greek! So, we know that Jesus was most assuredly tri-lingual, He spoke three languages!

You will find that there is a bias against Hebrew in many of the Biblical translations. In fact, in one translation, every time the word 'Hebrew' appears in the New Testament, the translators say the language is Aramaic, then they put a footnote at the bottom of the page that says, "or Hebrew." Hebrew and Aramaic are totally different words in Greek. They had concluded that no one spoke Hebrew during the time of Jesus.

Here are some of the confirmations that Hebrew was the dominant language. What was the sign put over the head of Jesus when He was crucified, *"Jesus of Nazareth, King of the Jews"* John 19:19. What three languages was it written in, according to the Books of Luke and John? The three languages were Greek, Latin, and Hebrew, not Aramaic, but Hebrew! If everyone was speaking Aramaic, why would they write it in Hebrew?

---

9. www.wikipedia.com, Talmud.

The fact that it was written in Hebrew shows that Hebrew was widely used as the written, read, and spoken language of Israel.

Another example of Jesus using Hebrew, was when He was on the cross and He cried out, *"Eli, Eli, lama sabachthani?"* The translators of Mark put, *"Eloi, Eloi, lama sabachthani,"* which totally destroys the whole meaning, and makes no sense whatsoever! *"Eloi"* is Aramaic, *"Eli"* is Hebrew. *"Lama,"* which means *"Why,"* is the same in both languages. *"Sabachthani,"* also the same in both languages, so it could be either one.[10] Therefore, how do we know which one is correct? In Matthew 27:47, we find the clue! Those standing around said, *"This man is calling for Elijah."* That statement could only be made if Jesus was speaking Hebrew, because in Aramaic the word for Elijah does not sound like *"Eli"* or *"Eloi." Eli* in Hebrew is short for Elijah, which is *Eliyahu. "Eli, Eli"* is "My God, My God." Jesus was quoting Psalm 22, *"My God, my God, why have You forsaken Me?"* Even on the cross, Jesus was quoting Scripture! Psalm 22, written by David hundreds of years before the crucifixion, describes what Jesus was experiencing on the cross!

In Acts 21:40, Paul was about to be arrested, he turned and spoke to the crowd in their own language, and it shocked them! What language was he speaking? He was speaking in Hebrew! If Paul was speaking Aramaic, that would not have been a shock to anyone! Paul was not a Jerusalem Jew, he was from *Tarsus*, and the crowd would have expected him to speak Aramaic.

Many things from that time period, such as

---

10. Bivin, David, *Understanding the Difficult Words of Jesus*, p. 10.

Temple coins, inscriptions on bone boxes, and prayers, were written in Hebrew. This shows us that Hebrew was the main language used during Jesus' time. Despite what many of the present-day scholars say, or what many seminaries teach, when we look at our scriptures like detectives, we see that <u>they are wrong</u>! Understanding the language of Jesus' day is an important fact for this study.

Papias, Bishop of Hierapolis, an early Christian father, stated that he had seen the original Gospel by Matthew. He explained that Matthew had put down the words of the LORD in the Hebrew language, in an ordered arrangement and each person has translated it the best he could![11] Why? Because they were writing for the people that spoke Greek, so they were having to translate it from Hebrew into the Greek language!

Thus, we see there was an original manuscript written by the disciple Matthew that was used in the writings of the Gospels. Luke, who did research, certainly used this document! The book of Matthew, that we have today, was most likely translated into Greek from the original Gospel of Matthew. Why would the original Gospel of the life of Jesus be written in Hebrew? Because everyone spoke Hebrew! The existence of this Hebrew text was confirmed by Eusebius and Jerome, and other early Christian Fathers. Jerome stated that the original copy was preserved in the library at Caesarea.[12]

---

11. Bivin, David, *Understanding the Difficult Words of Jesus*, pp. 23-25.
12. Bivin, David, *Understanding the Difficult Words of Jesus*, p. 25.

THE LANGUAGE OF THE GOSPELS

Remember Luke? He wrote to a Greek audience. He knew that he had to explain the Scripture and he didn't want them to miss the meaning. The language outside of Jerusalem, outside of Judea, was predominantly Greek. As for Paul, he wrote to the Churches in an area we call the *diaspora,* the dispersed Jews all over the known world. He conversed with them in the language that they understood. The imagery Paul used, such as armor, portrayed the Roman armor, not Jewish armor, because he wanted to use illustrations of things they were familiar with. He used cultural references of the society in which they lived. The language in which they wrote was the language of the people they ministered to.

The Gospel of John shows very strong Hebraic roots, but most likely, John was written in Greek. Matthew and Mark, especially Matthew, shows very strong Hebrew roots. They were either originally written in Hebrew, or they were drawn from an original Hebrew text. As mentioned before, there was an original Hebrew text, Matthew, which our Gospels were drawn from. The Gospel of Mark, according to Papias and other early Christian fathers, was written by Mark, who was a scribe for Peter while he was preaching in Rome. He wrote down the sermons of Peter, and was faithful to the work that was given to him.[13] We need to remember that all Scripture is God breathed! God inspired those who wrote the Scriptures through His Holy Spirit! All through the Gospel of Mark, he said, "The Prophets

---

13. www.wikipedia.com, **Papias of Hierapolis, Gospel Origins.**

say...." lumping the prophecies from different prophets together, whereas, Matthew said "in the Book of Isaiah" or "in the Book of Jeremiah." Luke had the tendency to do the same thing, citing his sources. Mark wrote the way a preacher would speak, linking the prophecies together. By the way, the Rabbis refer to 'putting Scriptures together,' one after another as, 'Stringing Pearls.' What did Jesus say in Matthew 7:6? *"Don't cast your pearls before swine."* As growth in Scriptural understanding occurs, there will always be naysayers, people that will not accept the conclusions, especially if it challenges their way of thinking.

Certain customs of the time help us to understand some of the difficult passages in the Scriptures. Without it, we are guessing at what the full meaning is. This does not affect our salvation or our eternal destination, but hopefully, it will excite us about the Word of God and give us a zeal to understand our Scriptures more completely. Let me give you an example that God gave me! You have a field; it produces everything you could want! It's the most productive, fertile field, it's growing all sorts of wonderful vegetables and providing you with land and water. However, you don't know that just below the surface, there are fabulous treasures buried! When you are seeking and you find one of those treasures, does that diminish the value of the field for all its other purposes? No! It's still providing everything you need. It is still just as rich and wonderful as it ever was. You just have something magnificent to add to it!

What we are seeking to do, is find those hidden treasures. Sometimes we have to adjust a bit in our thinking. That is fine! It doesn't mean that what we know isn't valid, it just means that there is more to be discovered. God's Truth is like an onion, we peel off a layer, there's another layer, and another, and another. There are deeper layers of understanding. You may say, "The word means this." I may say, "But the word means that," and we may both be right. A single verse can mean multiple things, because God's Wisdom is much more than we can understand. God's Word is alive! It is the living Word!

CHAPTER THREE
FIRST TREASURES REVEALED

JEWISH EXPECTATIONS

This topic is very near and dear to my heart. You see, I was one of those students in seminary that believed the lie that Jesus was not the Messiah. When I was introduced to the Jewish Roots study, God had already turned my life around completely, but it answered so many questions like: Why didn't Jesus come right out and say very plainly, "I am the Messiah!"? He said things like, *"Well, what do you think? What do you see? What do you hear?"* The Jewish Roots showed me there was a reason that He did not come right out and say, "Yes, I am the Messiah." He used the teaching method called *remez*, which means to allude to. He talked about Himself in the third person, such as the *"Son of Man,"* the *"Green Tree,"* or the *"Stone."* When we search the Scriptures, we find that Isaiah 42:1-3 is the key to understanding why he did not come straight out and say it the way we Western or Greek thinkers would have liked Him to.

In seminary, I was introduced to the writings of Dr. Albert Schweitzer. He concluded that Jesus either was not the Messiah and was claimed to be so by His Disciples, or that He was the Messiah and didn't know it! This type of thinking was called the 'Messianic Secrets,' which started around 1901, by a German theologian named William Wrede. His work concluded that Jesus didn't want anyone to know that He was the Messiah. Wrede came to this conclusion from statements that Jesus made when He performed miracles, such as "Don't tell anyone!"

The problem is that this theory has been developed by the thinking of the western theologians of the 19th-21st centuries, not by those that understood the Hebrew community of the First Century. In fact, most of our Biblical interpretations of the Scriptures are based on a German concept of higher criticism. Also, this was a time of strong anti-Semitic thinking within Germany. The underlying principle was the development of criticism, which is based on invalidating any authority in Scripture. They may not have had that in mind, but that was the way the enemy twisted their conclusions. Not all German theologians followed suit; Karl Barth was a sound scholarly German theologian during that period.

Isaiah 42 shows us that if we want to understand Jesus, we have to think like a Jew! Not a Jew of today, but we have to think like a Jew of the First Century, like the Jewish Rabbis! Let's look at what Isaiah 42 says, and seek to understand it. God is speaking: "*Behold My Servant whom I uphold, My Elect One whom My soul delights! I have put My Spirit upon Him; He will bring forth justice to the Gentiles.*" The first part of this, we see quotes many times, "*Behold My Servant whom I uphold,*" meaning, 'The One I lift up, My Elect One, My chosen One in whom My soul delights.' The Rabbis knew that God was referring to the Messiah. When the Rabbis read this, they said, 'That's the Messiah, the Chosen Servant, the Elect One. God is going to be pleased with Him.'

How do we know that He is the Messiah? Look at what it says, "*I have put My Spirit upon Him. He will bring forth Justice...*" It doesn't say 'to the Jews,' it says "*to the Gentiles. He will not cry out, nor raise His voice, <u>nor cause</u>*"

<u>His voice to be heard in the street</u>." In verse 3, "*A bruised reed He will not break, and smoking flax He will not quench;*" this was the foundational Scripture that under-girded their entire Messianic expectations. The King that comes will be humble and meek. Zachariah 9:9, "*lowly and riding on a donkey.*" He's going to be a humble, meek, and gentle person, He's not going to be a bragger. In fact, He's not even going to raise His voice in the street, meaning He will not declare openly that He is the Messiah! What does it mean, "*A bruised reed He will not break?*" He will be so gentle that when He walks by a flower that has a broken stem, He won't even make the flower fall off! "*A smoking flax...*" would be like the wick of a candle that smolders and becomes ash, if you even breathe on it, it scatters. The scripture is referring to the burnt wick of a lamp. The lamps of that day had twisted cloth in them to soak up the olive oil. Isaiah was saying that the Messiah wouldn't even quench the flame on a smoking flax, because He was so gentle, He wouldn't even scatter the ashes.

Remember, Jewish expression is extreme. You also see here some of what is called a Hebrew doublet, or parallelism. This is a form of literature that was very common in Jewish writing. They would repeat what they were saying, yet slightly different the second time for emphasis. In Proverbs 6:16, we find a perfect example of this, "*Six things God hates and seven He abhors,*" "*A bruised reed He will not break,*" and "*A smoking flax He will not quench.*" Isaiah is saying the same thing here; it's just stated slightly different the second time. There are doublets all through the Psalms, and Jesus sometimes used this pattern. He was very Hebraic in His language, His statements are often very poetic, such as

"Birds of the air..." and *"the flowers of the field."* It was the Jewish way, a very colorful, expressive language. Here's another Jewish way, everything starts with the word 'and.' *"And he said...,"* *"And God said..."* It's a Jewish way of linking things together. Jesus came as a Jew, He came with the expectations of the community around Him. He came to proclaim Himself the Messiah, but He knew that if He came right out saying, *"Okay everybody, I'm the Messiah,"* they would have rejected Him. Why? Isaiah 42:1-3 says, He had to come quietly, meekly, and proving who He was through His actions, and through His teachings, not by declaring Himself Messiah.

As a matter of fact, Rabbis went so far as to say, 'If someone comes declaring himself to be the Messiah, you know that he is not the Messiah.' Jesus accepted that. If someone said, *"I am the Christ,"* don't believe it, because when He comes you'll know it! You won't have to be told. Why? God will confirm it, be delighted in it, and you'll know it! Now, where is the text fulfilled one-hundred percent? Throughout the life of Jesus! If the Messiah did not declare it, how would they know who the Messiah was? Because of Isaiah 42:1-3. They knew their Scriptures; they knew the Messianic expectations.

Jesus generally did not directly claim to be the Messiah. However, there is one case that He did, to the woman at the well in Samaria, found in John 4, *"The Man you are talking to is He."* Why was that okay? She was not Jewish, she was a Samaritan, and she did not have the same expectations as the Jewish community did. The Samaritans only accepted the first five books of the Bible. They did not accept Isaiah or any of the Prophets. Why? Because the Prophets said Jerusalem was the place in which they must worship. The Samaritans worshipped at Mount Gerizim, where they claimed the original Holy Place was from the time that Joshua conquered Canaan, and the tribes of Israel settled the land. The Samaritans were Hebrews that had married Gentiles, thus they were considered half breeds by the Jews.   In John 4:20, the woman asked Jesus, *"Our fathers worshipped in these mountains, and you say...in Jerusalem..."* In other words, she was saying, 'You're getting too personal. Let's change the subject.' In doing evangelism, we find people will do this when the subject starts hitting too close to home. They will say something like, *"Oh! I've got a question about the Bible..."* That is a diversion, to get off the subject.

Jesus could reveal Himself as the Messiah to the woman at the well because she didn't have the same expectations that the Jews did. In most cases, however, what He did was give an indirect explanation: *"What do you hear? What do you see? You tell Me."* They asked Him at His trial, *"Are You the Messiah as they claim?"* He said, *"If I told you, you wouldn't believe Me. But if I asked you, you won't answer Me."*

MESSIANIC SIGNS

How would they know Jesus was the Messiah? There were <u>four Messianic signs</u> that the Rabbis had established, and people believed that only the Messiah could accomplish. Jesus did all these things and many still had trouble accepting Him as Messiah. When we read the New Testament, we recognize these signs because it says, "This has never been done in Israel before," or dispute it and say it didn't happen.

The four Messianic Signs are:
1: cast out a deaf/mute spirit.
2: heal a person that had been born blind.
3: heal a Jewish leper.
4: raise someone from the dead after more than three days and three nights.[14]

Let's look at each of the signs in more detail.
1: The casting out of a deaf/mute spirit. Jesus was not the only one to cast out spirits. In Luke 11:14-23, Jesus was accused of casting out demons by Beelzebub. His response was, *"If I cast them out by Beelzebub, by whose authority do your sons cast them out?"* When a person was under the anointing of the LORD, they could cast out spirits, whether it was Jesus or someone else. However, they had never been able to cast out a deaf/mute spirit. Why? They believed that they had to identify the spirit in order to call it by name and cast it out. If a person was deaf or mute, the demon could not give its name, as in Mark 9:14-32, the boy who was deaf/mute. The Disciples tried, but couldn't cast the spirit out. Jesus cast it out and this had never happened in Israel before. After the Sages looked through Scriptures and their own experiences, they said, 'When the Messiah comes, He will be able to do this.'

In Mark 6, Jesus sent out His disciples, two by two and mighty things happened, including exorcism. The people were saying, He is, "<u>The Prophet</u>," the one that Moses spoke of in Deuteronomy 18:15, 18:18-19.

---

14. Moseley, Dr. Ron, *Yeshua*, pp. 126-129.

God said to Moses, "*I will raise up for them, a Prophet like you from among their brethren…He shall speak…all I command.*" God went on and stated that anyone who did not hear His words and refused to accept Him, "*I will hold him accountable. He will be a Prophet like Moses.*" In the original Hebrew it said, 'the Prophet.' This expression became equivalent to the Messiah.

The Messiah would be the Prophet like Moses. Why? What was unique about Moses over all the other Prophets? Moses saw God face to face! Understand, this is an expression, in fact this expression has a name, it's called *four eyes*, meeting Face to face! It is a way of saying that Moses received his revelation directly from God.

In the Jewish writings, it states that they saw through the glass darkly. Does that sound familiar? In 1st Corinthians 13:12, it says, "*But now we see through a glass darkly, but then face to face.*" What does the expression, through a glass darkly mean? It means that the word of God is received in a vision or a dream. The word of God would come to them, but not as the audible voice of God Himself.

In their understanding, God Himself would come, sit down, and talk to His friend Moses. That's why Moses would glow with the glory of God around him, the *Shekinah*, the glory of God! God said, "*I'll show you a glimpse of My glory because you can't tolerate My full glory, you can't see Me and live.*" What does God do? He reveals Himself in such a way that Moses can tolerate it, but it's still so much that Moses comes out glowing. So, what does John 1:14 say about Jesus? "*We beheld His glory, the glory…of the Father.*" He is the glory of the Father, and no one has seen the Father but the Son. Jesus spoke with the Father face to face. We keep seeing this imagery declaring that Jesus is The Prophet, like Moses, who received his revelation directly from God, face to face. Jesus is, He who has seen the Father and tells us what the Father said.

2: The healing of a person born blind, remember the man born blind. In John 9, Jesus healed him. What did Jesus do to heal him? He spat on the ground, made mud, stuck it on his eyes, and then told him to go wash in the pool of Siloam.[15] By the way, did you ever stop and think about what's going on in that account? Why spit on the dirt and make mud? Does this remind you of the creation account in Genesis 2:7, *"And the LORD GOD formed man from the dust of the earth."* It is a creation miracle! Only God can create, that's why they said, no one could heal someone born blind but the Messiah, and His creative powers.

What did the Pharisees do to that man? They questioned him, and they did not believe that he had really been born blind. The man's parents were called in to testify. They stated that he had really been born blind! Then the Pharisees put the pressure on. John 9:22 states, *"if anyone confesses that He (Jesus) was the Christ, he would be put out of the Synagogue."* What were they saying? He would be excommunicated! That meant- being kicked out of the community, even the social life. So the parents told them to ask their son, he was an adult. The Pharisees questioned the man again. His response is found in John 9:27, *"Why do you want to hear it again? Do you want to also become His disciple?"* When Jesus heard that they had cast him out, He came up and asked him, *"Do you believe in the Son of God,"* John 9:35,36. He

---

15. www.wikipedia.com, Pool of Siloam.

replied, *"Who is He?"* Remember, the young man couldn't see, so he did not know who healed him! Jesus said in verse 37, *"…it is He that is talking with you."* The man said, *"LORD, I believe!"* Jesus does not directly say, I'm the Messiah! This is an example that is close to direct Proclamation, but He was speaking to someone who has already been excommunicated from the Synagogue.

3: The healing of a Jewish leper. In the Book of Leviticus, there are pages and pages of what a leper is to do when he is healed. The Priest was the one that had to declare a person a leper, unclean in the first place. To be declared clean, the person had to go back and be inspected by the Priest, according to the Law. The Priest inspected and would declare the person healed of leprosy. In all of their history, there had never been a record of a Jewish leper being healed.

In Numbers 12:1-15, God caused Miriam to become leprous for seven days. This was to teach her not to question God's servant, and it was before the setting up of the priestly line. What about Naaman? He was Syrian, he was not Jewish. The reference is found in 2nd Kings 5:1-17. They kept records in great detail, and there had never been a Jewish leper healed. The Rabbis determined that when Messiah comes, He would be able to heal a Jewish leper.

When the group of lepers saw Jesus, as recorded in Luke 17:12-19, they asked Him to heal them. He told them, *"Go show yourselves to the Priests."* It doesn't say that nine of them were Jews and one was a Samaritan; so, how do we know? Look at Jesus' words in verse 18, *"Were there not any found who returned to give glory to God except this foreigner?"* If the nine were not foreigners, then what does that say that they were? They were Jews that were healed. They were still lepers when they started out, but on the way to see the priest, they were healed. The Samaritan returned and began to praise God. Jesus asked, *"Where are the nine?"* Jesus was making the point, don't forget to praise God in the process. When the men got to the Temple, they would tell the Priest 'It was Yeshua, the Nazarene, He's the one that healed us.' God's power stands up to scrutiny. So the Priests made the decision, and declared the men healed, and the priest had to document that they were healed of leprosy.

4: Raising someone from the dead after more than three days and three nights. Understand this, the Jewish custom was, and still is, that they bury the person on the day that they died, within 24 hours of death. If they died that day, they were buried before sundown. If they died at night, they bury them before sundown the next day. The dead were wrapped in a shroud or linen. Actually, in those days, most were wrapped like a mummy, in winding cloth, and a small cloth was wrapped to hold the jaw together. Coins were sometimes placed over the eyes and they would often put flowers around the body. The *Shroud of Turin* shows that flowers were placed on the body, to mask some of the smells.[16] When they put the body in the tomb, they would place a rolling stone that looked like a big stone wheel to close the door to the tomb. Commonly, there was a trench for the stone to sit in, so it could roll back and forth easily. Inside, there would have been one or two slabs that the bodies would be laid on.

Each family member that died would be buried

---

16. *National Geographic*, June 1980, Vol 157, No 6, pp. 730-753.

in the same tomb. The family would come back in one year and gather the bones, and put them in a pile or, as in Jesus' days, a bone box called an *ossuary*.[17] An *ossuary* was about three and one half feet long, a little longer then a human femur, which is the longest bone in the human body. They might put the bones of several people in the same ossuary. This is called being <u>gathered to your people</u>. This is what was meant when we see "*gathered to his people*" in the Scriptures. A person who was crucified by the Romans was not only humiliated in life, but also in death. They were not allowed to be buried by their people in the family tomb. It was a way of punishing them after death.

    On occasion, when they went back a year later to gather the bones, they were not where they had laid them! The person had revived and tried to get out of the tomb. There were conditions that mimicked death and the person whom they entombed was not dead. A thought developed that for three days and three nights, the Spirit would hover over the body attempting to get back in. They developed a practice of going back to the tomb each day for three days after the person was buried. The family would roll the stone back, and call out the deceased's name. They would look and listen for any response, any movement at all. If there were no sounds, they would roll the stone back in place. After the <u>third day and the third night</u>, no one had ever moved, so three days and three nights came to mean - <u>really dead</u>.

    During the period of mourning, they would sit

---

17. *Biblical Archaeology Review*, July/August 2003, Vol 29, No 4. Keall, Edward J., Brother of Jesus Ossuary.

close to the floor, they would not wear comfortable clothing or comfortable shoes. They didn't eat comforting meals, wash, nor do normal daily activities, except on the Sabbath, when they were allowed to make themselves presentable. It was called sitting *Shiva*, mourning for seven days. The word *Shiva* means, sitting seven.[18]

In John 11:1-44, we find the account of Lazarus' death. In Hebrew, his name was *Lazar*, the '*us*' was a Greek addition. Jesus said that Lazar was sleeping. His disciples said, "*LORD, if he sleeps, he will get well.*" Jesus responded, "*Lazar is dead.*" Now, Jesus waited until the fourth day to arrive. Why? That way no one could say that it was a natural resuscitation, or that the Spirit was waiting to come back when *Lazar*'s name was called out. Jesus waited until the situation was considered beyond hope. That's why the sisters said to Him, "*If you had been here, my brother would not have died.*" Jesus said, "*I am the resurrection and the life.*" He told them, "*Take back the stone.*" Martha said, "*LORD, by this time there is a stench,*" in other words, it's beyond hope. Jesus did exactly what the family would have done. He rolled back the stone and said, "*Lazar, come forth.*" When God does it, things happens! What was really significant is that he was dead three days and three nights. Lazar was raised from the dead, but he was not resurrected. Lazar would die again, he was restored to a physical body, but Lazar experienced another death.

The resurrected body experiences no more death, and is never described as flesh and blood. It is always described as flesh and bone. Why? The life of the

---

18. Moseley, Dr. Ron, *Yeshua*, p. 180.

creature is in the blood, but what is the life in the resurrected body of Jesus? He is the Life, He doesn't need blood. A resurrected body doesn't have to eat or drink, but can. It is not limited by the physical limitations of this world. Why? The life is not in the blood, the life is in the LORD! We will be given a body like Jesus', meaning it will have appearance and be recognizable by our loved ones. It says in 1st Corinthians 13:12, *"We will know as we are known."*

It says in John 12:10, after Jesus raised Lazar from the dead, the Jews sought to kill Lazar because many people were coming to Jesus due to the raising of Lazar! Why would the people come to Jesus because of that? Because Lazar was a man that was dead, and Jesus brought him back to life, and they knew that only the Messiah could do that.

The expectations of the whole of Judea were the <u>Messianic Miracles</u>, miracles that only the Messiah could do. Jesus fulfilled them all and said in a Hebrew way, "Here I am!" Even with that evidence, there was a struggle in belief. The High Priest and many of the Priests, did not want to accept Jesus as Messiah, because it was political suicide for them to embrace the reality. It would upset their arrangement with the Romans. Remember there were 50,000-80,000 believers in the Jerusalem area alone by 70 AD. From the common people to the Pharisees, they had embraced Jesus as their Messiah.

JESUS AS A BOY

One of my favorite examples of Jesus proclaiming Himself Messiah is found in Luke 2:41-50. Jesus was twelve-years-old and the family was in Jerusalem for Passover, they were very righteous people. It was a very expensive trip, but they went *"every year"* and brought their sacrifices. They were not rich people, but they knew how important it was to keep the Law. The Law said in Deuteronomy 16:16, *"...your males shall appear before the* L{\sc ord} *your God..."* So, even as a young child, Jesus kept the Law. The trip from Nazareth to Jerusalem was about seventy miles; they would travel in a large company, probably cousins, friends and neighbors. There was safety in numbers from robbers. They were on their way back after the Passover, they have traveled a day's journey from Jerusalem. It was sundown, suppertime, and Jesus didn't show up. They looked around, they asked everyone, no one had seen Him. Jesus wasn't with them, and they were in a panic.

Jesus was a twelve-year-old boy in a huge city. The city of Jerusalem had a normal population of 80,000-150,000 people at that time, but a tremendous crowd were there during the Passover season, as many as two million people. It is one of the three God ordained feasts, and Jews would travel from all over the known world for the feast. It would have been easy for a young boy to get separated from His family.

Joseph and Mary traveled a day's journey back to Jerusalem and on the third Day, <u>on the third day</u> again, they went to the Temple, and there He sat very calmly. They were probably sitting in the Royal Portico, which was to the south, in the covered area where Rabbis would sit, debate, and discuss Scripture. Jesus was sitting there talking to the Rabbis in Hebrew and discussing Scripture at such a level of understanding that they were amazed at His wisdom.

By William Hallmark ©

It says in verses 46, 47 "...*asking them questions, and all...were astonished at His understanding and answers.*" Do you see something strange about that statement? He was asking them questions and they were amazed at His answers. There is a clue here. This was one of the teaching techniques that was used by the Rabbis when dealing with a sophisticated student.

A renowned Jewish Roots teacher, Dwight A. Pryor, referred to this form of discussion in the teachings as *Question for Question*. The way the process worked is this: Either the Rabbi starts out or the student starts out by asking a question. Now, they didn't answer the question, they would ask another question, which assumes the answer of the first question, taking it to a deeper level. They didn't respond with an answer, they responded back with another question. This would go on until it reached the level of the total understanding of the student. It took the student as far as he could go, then the Rabbi knew exactly how much the student knew.[19]

So, when it says that "*He asked them questions and they were amazed at His answers,*" it means that He was engaged in Question for Question process. They were amazed that Jesus had such great wisdom and insight for a boy of only twelve years. The Rabbis and Jesus had been engaged in this process for three days. They were in absolute awe of this Boy. When His parents arrived, His mother said, "*Son why have you done this to us?*" Jesus answered them saying, "*Did you not know that I must be about My Father's business?*" Now, that had to have blown the Rabbis away. Jesus said, "*In My Father's house,*" or "*About My Father's business,*" depending on the translation. Both of those translations have been found in some ancient fragments. Both of them were really saying the same thing. What is His Father's business? The Jews said that God was the great Teacher who sat down with Moses and began to teach him the Law. So, the Son takes up His Father's occupation, teaching the Word in "*My Father's house.*" Where were they? They were in the Temple, and it was called 'The House of God, God's House, and The House.' Either way, there was no question who Jesus was talking about. He was talking about God, correct? Remember, Messiah is called the Son of God, based on Psalm 2, it is one of the key Messianic verses, "*You are My Son. Today I have begotten You.*" Everyone called God, *Father*, because God was the LORD Kinsman, the Head of the

---

19. Stern, David H., *Jewish New Testament Commentary*, p. 110.

House, and every Jew was His child, so they called Him *'Avinu' (ah Vee nu)*, <u>Our Father</u>. The Rabbis had said that only the Messiah would have such a personal relationship that He could call God *'Avi,' (ah Vee), My Father*. So, when Jesus answered His mother, "*Did you not know I must be in <u>My Father's</u> house*" in front of all of the Rabbis, they must have wondered, He said *'My Father!'* He had shown His great wisdom of Scripture and the traditions of the great Rabbis. He knew no one was to call God, My Father! Why would He have said that? There must have been great confusion, but Mary treasured it and "*kept all these things in her heart.*" She must have been thinking, 'Oh yes! You are the Son of God!'

    The point is, Jesus declared that He was Messiah when He said, "*My Father!*" There is no question, He did not make a mistake, Jesus knew that He was the Anointed One, the Messiah, and this makes it very clear. That's what confused the Rabbis, they must have been wondering, 'Did He just call Himself the Messiah. He must have made a mistake, but He's been so wise. He knows so much!' You see the confusion it would have created? Some people say that Jesus didn't know He was the Messiah, but as we see here, He knew at the age of twelve. Though He didn't walk in it until He reached the age of thirty, not until the Spirit descended upon Him. Why? He was absolutely obedient to the Law of God, His commands, which means He was an obedient Son. He didn't do anything His Father wouldn't want Him to do, He didn't say anything His Father didn't say. He had His Father's power, His Father's miracles, and His Father's knowledge. Philippians 2:5-8 tells us He gave up His equality with God and took on the form of a man and became fully human. So how did He know what people were thinking? What someone's name was? What to do? Whom to heal? What to say? Remember all the times in Scripture that it says, Jesus rose up early to be alone and pray, or sent the disciples ahead, and he went aside to pray. He was constantly speaking with His Father, to know His will. He was the perfectly obedient Son. He was what Adam should have been. Adam should have been the obedient son, but he chose disobedience over obedience. That is why sin came through Adam, not through Eve. She was deceived. Adam knew exactly what he was doing, and he chose disobedience over the will of the Father. So the second Adam, the last Adam, chooses obedience in order to undo what the first Adam did.

HIS MESSIANIC CLAIM

In Luke 19, we find the account of Zacchaeus, which is filled with imagery. We see an account of Zacchaeus' transformation in life and the declaration of his intent to repay those he has wronged. In Luke 19:9-10, Jesus said, *"Today salvation has come to this house. For this man too is a son of Abraham. For the Son of Man has come to seek and to save that which is lost."* When Jewish listeners of the First Century heard that, it blew them away! Jesus was not only claiming His Messiah-ship, but He also declared Himself to be God! How does He do that? Where does *Son of Man* come from, Daniel 7:13-14. Commit Daniel 7:13,14 to memory; it is the foundation principle of the Son of Man.

Jesus combines His favorite title for Himself, Son of Man, with a passage from Ezekiel Chapter 34. In Ezekiel God basically said, 'I am sick and tired of My Shepherds. They have fed themselves and let My people starve, and scattered My people!' Then He said in verses 11, 12-16, 22-25: *'I Myself will put My servant David over them,'* but David is dead! So what does *"My servant David"* mean? God is saying He will put Messiah over them! But who is going to seek and save the lost? God said, 'I will do this Myself.' Why does Jesus say that The Son of Man has come to do what God Himself said only He will do? In other words, 'I am God coming to do this job.' Now, Jesus made a declaration of His Divinity as well as a declaration of Messiahship with that statement using *remez*. The meaning of Remez is: to hint or allude to.[20]

When people say Jesus never claimed to be Messiah, they do not understand the scriptures. He said it all the time, but He said it in a First Century Jewish way. Now, hopefully you can see that He did it in a way that the people would understand. When they heard that, their minds went straight to Ezekiel. I am sure they were thinking, 'But God said He was going to save the lost. Now Jesus said that He's here to save the lost. That's what God said, "I Myself will do." 'Could this be God?' That was a tremendous declaration, but we miss it if we don't search the Old Testament for what Jesus was really saying.

Jesus implied the same thing in John 15:20; 'If they do this to the Master of the house, what will they do to the servant?' Master of the house does not mean

---

20. Stern, David H., *Jewish New Testament Commentary*, p. 12.

the head of the house. The House is an expression for the Temple, and God was called the Master of the House, the LORD of the House, and Jesus was equating Himself to the Master of the House. "*If they persecute Me, they will also persecute you.*" In several places, Jesus calls Himself God very clearly, in a Jewish way. That's why the Sadducees and Pharisees who opposed Him, accused Him of blasphemy, 'You, a mere Man, make Yourself to be God!'

Do you see how He understands Himself and knew full well that He was Messiah? But He had to present Himself in a way that the Jewish people of the First Century would understand and accept. Our problem is that we have lost this through time and through the strong anti-Semitic attitudes within the Church. The anti-Semitic attitude goes back so far in our history that it is to the point that we don't even see it! We need to rediscover Jesus' revelation and the understanding of Himself as a First Century Jew, so that when people say He wasn't the Messiah, we can answer them in a non-emotional way, with facts!

The accounts I have shared are from the Gospels, and they show how Jesus presented Himself, always in a Jewish way, so that His Jewish audience would listen and understand. Why is that important? These are the people that Jesus was sent to, to gather a body from, to gather His Disciples from. If He had done things that were offensive to the Jews of that day, if He had come right out and said, "I'm the Messiah," no one would have listened to Him.

What was the temptation when Satan took Jesus to the pinnacle of the Temple, to the high point of the Temple Mount, 'Jump off and prove to everyone who

You are,' Matthew 4:5-7. The Jews believed that when Messiah came, He would appear on the pinnacle of the Temple.[21] Satan was tempting Jesus to do it His way, not God's way, to *"make His voice heard in the streets."* When Jesus did things, He did them quietly, even with the miracles He performed. In Jesus' actions, He was saying, 'I don't want to be known for the miracles I perform, I want people to hear My message and to recognize Me as their Messiah.'

Jesus makes it plain, He has come to the Jews. This is very obvious in Matthew 15: 21-28. A woman from Canaan came to Jesus and cried out *"Have mercy on me, O Lord, Son of David! My daughter is demon-possessed."* Jesus answered her, *"I was not sent except to the lost sheep of the house of Israel."* She replied, *"LORD, help me!"* He answered her, *"It is not good to take the children's bread and throw it to the dogs."* Why is He calling her a dog? That was a reference to Gentiles, and she was not offended. It means a pet dog, not a pack of wild dogs. It's still a putdown, but it was a common one. What was He saying? 'I came for the Jews. I didn't come for the Gentiles. In time, My Father will go to the Gentiles, but My job is to build a body out of the Jews, to be My witnesses. They understand the concept of Messiah and they are waiting for Me to come.' She stated, *"Yes, but even the dogs get to eat the crumbs that fall from the table."* So Jesus proclaimed how great her faith was and delivered her daughter.

---

21. Young, Brad H., *Jesus the Jewish Theologian*, p. 31.

CHAPTER FOUR
NUGGETS OF TRUTH

JESUS' BAPTISM

At the baptism of Jesus, John testified to whom Jesus was when he said, *"Behold the Lamb of God,"* John 1:29. Jesus came to John to be baptized, not for the forgiveness of sin but to begin His ministry. We know what Jewish baptism was like and it wasn't done the way any of us do baptisms today. Jesus was immersed the way the *Talmud* defines immersion. The one being baptized immersed themselves. John would have stood on the bank, observing to make sure every hair on Jesus' head went under the water. Jesus would have put himself under the water three times. That was the common practice of baptism in Jesus' time.

Ritual baptism was originally for cleansing, but under John, baptism changed from a symbolic act to meet the requirement of the Law, to a personal response to God. John focused on being baptized with <u>repentance for the forgiveness of sins</u>.[22] Everyone who came to be baptized, was identifying with John's message and becoming a disciple of John's. That is why John said in John 3:30, *"He must increase, but I must decrease."* He recognized that his job had been fulfilled, the forerunner to the Messiah. That was a major revision from the way baptism was done.

The Hebrew definition of *Baptize* meant literally to be cleansed, to be permeated inside and out, a total cleansing. The word comes from the act of dipping cloth

---

22. Bean, William E., *New Treasures*, pp. 99-101.

in dye. When the cloth is brought out of the dye, it is still the same cloth, but it is totally changed. <u>It had now taken on itself the nature of the thing in which it was dipped</u>.[23] Baptism was used by Jews for an inestimable period. The Dead Sea Scrolls speak of immersion.[24] It was for ritual purity in order to go before the LORD on the Temple Mount. It was not discussed, like many things of that time period, because it was just part of their normal lives, and every Jew had been baptized many times. *Mikveh* is the Hebrew word for baptismal pool, *Mikva'ot* is the plural. The *Mikva'ot* at the Temple Mount were discovered by archeologists on the south side, between the triple doors and the double doors.[25] That was probably the Priests' entrance, next to the granary. That was where people went in to be ritually cleansed before they could go on to the Temple Mount. People who were financially able would have their own *Mikveh* in their homes for the purpose of ritual cleansing, usually on the rooftop. I believe Bathsheba was coming from her *Mikveh* when David saw her, 2nd Samuel 11. We know that the Essenes, Pharisees, and Rabbis had their own private *Mikveh*, which had to have at least 150 gallons of water.[26] In Jewish understanding, water represented the Holy Spirit, so it had to be living water, water that flows in and out by itself. That's why Baptizing in a river or lake was preferred.[27] They would go under three times.

---

23. Stern, David H., *Jewish New Testament Commentary*, p. 15.
24. Young, Brad H., *Jesus the Jewish Theologian*, p. 13-26.
25. www.ritmeyer.com, Ritmeyer Archaeological Design, Temple Mount Mikveh.
26. www.wikipedia.com, Mikveh, Requirements.
27. Tverberg, Lois and Okkema, Bruce, *Listening to the Language of the Bible*, p. 39.

The early Church, being Jewish, took the triple immersion to be their form of baptism, an act of their own volition. It had symbolism to them of their accepting Jesus as their Messiah. It was a given that one had to be baptized. Why? Not in order to be saved, it was a public declaration. It was a believer's baptism, because all these people, the first group of people to follow Jesus, were Jews. They had already been circumcised, they were part of the family of God. They were identifying with who Jesus was, His message, and becoming a disciple of Jesus. They saw their baptism as an essential part of becoming the covenant community.

Paul at Ephesus asked in Acts 19:3, "*Into what were you baptized?*" They answer, "*into John's.*" Paul tells them that they have to be willing to publicly identify with Jesus and His Message, the person and the promise. One of those promises was and is that He would baptize with the Holy Spirit. Jesus was the medium in which they were being baptized, the water is not important, the mode is not important. We are choosing to be baptized into Jesus, like the cloth, taking on His nature, His character, His quality. It is the defining stamp of whom Jesus is, in our lives.

I have heard it said that baptism is the equivalent of circumcision. No! The men of the early church had been circumcised as infants, yet they chose and desired to be baptized. When a Gentile converted to Judaism, he was circumcised and baptized. When they came out of the water, it was like it was the first day of their lives, like they had been Born Again! They were no longer a Gentile; they were a Son of Israel!

Do you see why baptism is so important? It became important in the life of the early Church. All of this symbolism and all of this meaning has its origin in the customs of their time, in the Jewish community. Baptism has no power to save but it was so much a part of the process of becoming a part of the body, not joining a church. That is what it has become today. They became part of <u>the Church,</u> since there was only one body that accepted Jesus as the Messiah. They were baptized in His name and they became a part of the covenant community. It was done as a believer and as a statement of faith.

At Jesus' baptism, what is the conformation? Matthew 3:17 states that a voice came from heaven saying, "<u>This is My beloved Son, in whom My soul delights.</u>" "*My beloved Son*" comes from Psalm 2:7, "*You are My Son. Today I have begotten You.*" What does the Spirit appear as? John sees it as a dove, a bodily dove, descending and coming to rest on Jesus. The Scripture says in Isaiah 42:1, "*I have put My Spirit upon Him.*" In Matthew 12:18, the fulfillment of that Scripture came at His baptism. In John's mind, it was confirmed. John knew for sure, there was no question in his mind at all. John knew that Jesus was the Chosen One, the Elect One.

There is no evidence that anyone else understood God's words, or that anyone else saw the vision but John and the Son of God. We don't know, because the text does not say that anyone else understood it. They may have heard a rumbling. In Exodus 20:18, it tells us that when God spoke the Ten Commandments at Mt. Sinai, the Israelites heard the sound of thundering and the trumpet. In Paul's encounter with Jesus, he carried on a conversation with the light, the other people were untouched. Revelation can come in the midst of others, but only the one or two experience the revelation.

How old was Jesus when He was baptized? He had to be thirty-years-old. Why? Because of a Jewish requirement, He could not be a Rabbi until age 30, when He comes into His fullness. At the age of 5, boys started studying the Scripture. At 13, boys become an adult, because they have memorized the *Torah*. At 18, they were ready to marry, and pursue their manual occupation at age 20. At the age of 30, they came into their fullness, the age they had to be to become a Rabbi. At 40, they could be an elder in the Synagogue. At 50, they came into their wisdom and they were ready to council the younger people. This was understood by the people of that time, there were established age stages in life.[28]

IDIOMS

By using the information that we have gained concerning the language that was spoken, let's look at Matthew 6:19-24, part of what we call 'The Sermon on the Mount.' It says, "*Do not lay up for yourselves treasures on earth where moths and rust destroy and thieves break in and steal.*" To better understand this statement, we need to understand the customs and culture of that day! What does it mean? 'Don't lay up your treasures on earth where moths and rust destroy and thieves break in and steal.' What do you think moths and rust have to do with treasures?

In First Century Judea, there were three ways in

---

28. Edersheim, Alfred, *Sketches of Jewish Social Life*, pp. 100-101.
Bivin, David, *New Light on the Difficult Words of Jesus*, p. 4.

which to value a person's wealth: What kind of clothing they wore; how much money they had; and how much land or things they possessed.

1. How many times have we read, "And the man wore fine linen." That was like saying he was wealthy, well to do. That was one of the main ways they measured a person's wealth, by the clothing they wore. What do moths destroy? "Clothing."

2. What does rust destroy? What was money made of in those days? It was made of metal. Coins were struck in various metals, some with silver, some with gold, but most common coins were a mixture of metals! They didn't do a very good job of smelting in those times.

Photo by Ethan McCoy ©

The most common way of storing money was in clay jars and burying it in the ground. Depending on the moisture in the ground and how long it was left there, when the jar was retrieved, the money may have been reduced to a handful of rust! Rust eroded the coins and made them worthless. It may not have destroyed it completely, but it reduced the original weight of the coins, which destroyed its value.

3. Property or possessions are easy for us to understand. Thieves can always find a way to take possessions.

What's the point here? Hoarding up money doesn't work. We hoard treasures for ourselves, then what can happen? The moths can eat our clothing, the rust can destroy our money, and thieves can break in and steal our property, and our possessions. A person can lose their treasures on earth through any number of ways.

Jesus continues *"But lay-up yourself treasures in heaven."* Understand this, *'In heaven'* is literally plural. It is the word *'shamayim.'* It literally means, 'in the heavens!' Meaning 'in your relationship with God, who is supernatural!' In other words, Jesus was saying, lay up treasures in your relationship with God! Jesus was not talking about where we're going when we die, He was talking about our relationship with God.

Jesus continues, *"Where neither moths nor rust destroy, and thieves break in and steal."* No one can destroy our relationship with God but us. Then He said, *"For where your treasure is, there your heart will be also."* That which you prize the most, that's what you'll be committed to. That's where your heart is going to be, your love, right? You have to make a choice, what you're going to value the most. What you treasure, you're going to value; so if you treasure things on earth, that's what you'll value. If you treasure your relationship with God, that's what you're going to value.

Let's skip down to verse 24, *"No one can serve two*

masters, for either he will hate the one and love the other; or else he will be loyal to one, and despise the other. You cannot serve God and mammon." Mammon is a Hebrew word that means Material Wealth, Riches! So, He was saying that we cannot serve two masters. We will either hate the one and love the other or will cling to the one and despise the other. We cannot serve both God and earthly possessions! So which are you going to serve?

Now, I want to go back to verses 22 and 23, *"The lamp of the body is the eye. If therefore your eye is good, your whole body will be full of light. But if your eye is bad, your whole body will be full of darkness. If therefore, the light that is in you is darkness, how great is that darkness!"* Notice in verses 19 through 21, He's talking about treasures. In verse 24, He's talking about treasures, but in-between, He's talking about the lamp of the body being the eye! That seems to makes no sense! What was Jesus saying here?

Commentary after commentary has tried to make sense of these verses. The New International Version has actually changed it to plural trying to make it fit: *"The lamp of the body are your eyes, and if your eyes are good..."* It's not plural, it's singular. What does it mean? Some of the commentaries go into, "It's the window of the soul!" The problem is, everyone is speculating. No-one stopped to think that it could be found in the Old Testament. Why? New Testament Scholars study Greek, the language the New Testament comes to us in. The Old Testament scholars study Aramaic and Hebrew. This is the problem; they have not shared with each other in the past. I hope that has changed.

Let me shed some light on the subject by introducing you to the works of scholar, Dr. Robert L.

Lindsey. He was a Baptist missionary who pastored the Narkis Street Baptist Church in Jerusalem and was fluent in both Greek and Hebrew. His congregation spoke Hebrew, and the text they were using was translated from German to Hebrew! He decided to translate the New Testament from the Greek into Hebrew. When Dr. Lindsey started that project, he started making discoveries! One of the discoveries he made was when he translated the Gospels into Hebrew, he found that the words of Jesus flowed so much more smoothly! Mark was especially a very poor read in Greek, but when Dr. Lindsey put it into Hebrew syntax, which is language structure, it fit! He discovered that the Hebrew was underlying the Greek! In other words, it was written in Hebrew, then translated into Greek, not the other way around, as it has been taught for centuries. As he started looking at it, his discoveries were awesome. In Proverbs 22:9, it read something to this effect, *"He who has a generous eye will be blessed, for he gives of his bread with the poor."* It's not translated as '<u>the good eye</u>', but that's what it says in the Hebrew. It uses *"The bountiful man," "The generous man," "The merciful man will be blessed, for he shares his goods with the poor, his bounty with the poor."*

    This phrase, a 'good eye' is an <u>idiom</u>![29] Now, do you understand what an idiom is? The definition of an idiom is: An expression in a language that differs from its literal meaning. English is full of idioms! One of my favorites is, "I'll keep an eye out for you." Translate that into another language for someone that does not understand our language or our culture, they are going

---

29. Bivin, David, *Understanding the Difficult Words of Jesus*, p. 104.

to think we're mutilators! Some other idioms are: "Keep an ear to the ground," "He's a pain in the neck," "Get off my back," "Hold down the fort," or "Straight from the horse's mouth." We know what they mean because we use them in our language. Every culture has its idioms, its own expressions. They are expressions that once had logical meanings but have now taken on a definition that is no longer literal. An idiom cannot be translated literally or else the meaning is lost!

Hebrew is a very colorful language and is full of idiom. [30] One of the reasons idioms were used extensively was because Hebrew had very few adjectives. With very few adjectives, they made the language more colorful by combining words in unique ways and coming up with special meanings, and Hebrew does this over and over again.

The *aiyin tovah,* which means 'the eye is good' or 'the eye that is good,' is a Jewish idiom for a generous person. The generous person looks out and sees the needs of others. He looks beyond himself. He is like his Father who looks out with mercy and sees the needs of His children! Therefore, he looks with a 'good eye.' An eye that seeks good! So the expression, 'the good eye' became a way of saying: A generous, kind, merciful, person sees the needs of the others and gives to their needs.

Proverbs 22:9 says, *"He who has a good eye will be blessed because he shares his goods, his wealth with the poor."* Deuteronomy 15:9 says, *"If your eye be evil..."* the *aiyin ra'ah* in Hebrew, you will not show pity for those in

---

30. Bivin, David, *New Light of the Difficult Words of Jesus*, pp. xxv-xxvi.

need. We find many expressions similar to this in Scripture. The idea of the 'eye' doesn't literally mean the person's eye; basically, the eye is one's attitude. What attitude do we have toward other people? That's determined by our 'eye.' Now, if the 'good eye' looks out and sees the needs of others, what do you think the 'evil eye' does? The 'evil eye' looking inward, concerned about the needs of 'Self,' which can also include getting even with others or doing harm to others. What are the primary motivations of the 'evil eye' person? Self-centered-ness! Self-promotion! Greed! Fear! Greed says, "Whatever I have, it's not enough!" Fear says, "I might not have it when I need it, so I have to hoard it! I have to keep it back!" In other words, "I can't trust God to provide it! I've got to protect myself!" That's fear! What does Jesus say about that person? "That person is full of darkness, he is blind!" Whereas, the person with the 'good eye' is like his Father, who is full of light and mercy![31]

Now, let's put that into context: 'Don't store up your treasures on earth where they can be destroyed. Store up your treasures in your relationship with God. For if you are a generous person, you are full of light and it affects your whole being. When you serve God, the riches are a tool in your hand, and it's a blessing! It's a joy, because you're not bound by it and you are generous like your heavenly Father. You cannot serve two masters. If you are a selfish person, it affects your whole being. If you serve riches, it will control you, and you will not be free to serve God!

In conclusion, you cannot be stingy and be part

---

31. Cohen, Abraham, *Everyman's Talmud*, pp. 270-271.

of the Kingdom of God! This is the lesson hidden in the idiom of 'the good eye.' Unless we recognize the Hebrew and start looking at the Hebrew under-girding of the text, we will not catch that this is an idiom, an expression, and therefore we miss the meaning. By rediscovering the Hebrew that underlies it, we begin to unlock some of these difficult passages.

FULFILLING THE LAW

I want to share what some consider a very controversial text. In Matthew 5:17, Jesus was speaking during His Sermon on the Mount, He said, *"Do not think that I came to destroy the Law or the Prophets, I did not come to destroy* (or abolish), *but to fulfill"* the Law. Now, when something is fulfilled, we think of it as completed, right? In Romans 10:4, didn't Paul say that Jesus is the end of the Law? Does this mean it's done away with? No, that's not what it means at all. First of all, the word that says Jesus is the end of the law, *telos,* does not just mean 'the end,' it means the goal, the purpose!

Jesus was what the Law was pointing to, aiming at! He was the Man who walked in perfect obedience, in perfect relationships! Jesus is the fulfillment of what the Law was trying to get people to be! It doesn't mean that Jesus came and said, "The Law is over and done with, throw it away, burn it!" In fact, in Matthew 5:18 he said, *"...till heaven and earth pass away, one jot or one tittle will by no means pass from the Law..."* It is apparent here what Jesus' attitude toward the Law was. Remember, always read the scriptures surrounding a verse. The verse does not stand alone; it must be taken in context.

The terms that are used for 'abolish/destroy and fulfill' are classic Rabbinic terms that are found in Rabbinic writings. This is what the Rabbis understood these terms to mean: To abolish the Law or destroy the Law means to give it a false interpretation, to interpret it incorrectly! To fulfill the Law, therefore, meant to give it a correct interpretation. Let me share an example: Two Rabbis get into an argument over how to interpret a text. One of them said, "You're destroying the Law!" The other replies, "No I'm not. I'm fulfilling it!" This was how the people who heard Jesus speak, understood it. He had come to interpret the Law correctly![32]

What was Jesus getting ready to do in Matthew 5? He was getting ready to explain His teachings on the Sermon on the Mount. He's getting ready to give a re-interpretation of the Law and explain what God had in mind when He first gave the Law! "*You've heard it said ..., but I say to you,*" in other words, Jesus was saying, 'this is what it means, you need to understand this, I'm not here to mislead you, I'm here to show you what God has been telling you all along, what God had in mind when the Law was spoken!' All His listeners understood exactly what He was saying, 'I'm going to give you a proper interpretation!' If we take the surface meaning, it still has meaning: 'I'm not here to destroy the Law. I'm here to make it fulfilled, I'm here to make it happen.' Remember, Scripture is God's Living Word and there are new revelations for us every time that we read them.

Some say, 'we're under grace, we're not under

---

32. Bivin, David, *Understanding the Difficult Words of Jesus*, pp. 111-118.

Law.' In Jeremiah 31:33, where does it say God is going to write the Law? On our heart! We are supposed to have the Law in our hearts. This means it becomes our motivation to do, not something imposed on us! It becomes our desire! That doesn't mean the ritual aspects of the Law, it means the Spirit of the Law. Jesus summarized the Spirit of the Law well, "<u>Love God, and Love others</u>." The whole of Law is relationships: with God and with others. Every Law that God gave, all 613 of them, deal with either our relationship with God, formal or informal content, or our relationship with other people, either formal or informal content. Life is about relationships.

Jesus was saying, 'Not the smallest letter, not even the little decorations on the letters are going to pass away, until everything has been accomplished.' Now that's neat when you think about it! Jesus goes on and He said that, 'Heaven and Earth will pass away, but My Law, My words will not.' He instituted the Word so He is the Lawgiver. God didn't say, "Aw, the Law didn't work, throw it out. Let's start all over again." There's continuity here! Jesus is the very living Law, the living *Torah*! He is the embodiment of what *Torah* means!

What does He mean by a jot and a tittle? Here is a little trivia that I love. The "*jot*" actually refers to the smallest letter in the Hebrew alphabet, which is the *Yod*, and it is written like an apostrophe, just like a little apostrophe. The smallest letter in the Hebrew alphabet, and He was saying, 'not even the smallest letter in the alphabet will pass away before everything is fulfilled.'[33] "Tittle" refers to something called the *Kotz*. Now, *kotz*

---

33. Bivin, David, *Understanding the Difficult Words of Jesus*, p. 115.

literally means thorn, and refers to the decorations that were put at the top of some of the letters in Hebrew. It is also sometimes called the crown made up of thorns. *Kotz* means thorn, and <u>they crown the Word with thorns</u>![34] It is a crown of thorns on certain letters of the Word. John 1:14 tells us, *"And the Word became flesh and dwelt among us."* Jesus was the Word that became flesh and He was crowned with a crown of thorns at His crucifixion! I love this little jewel of information.

Here's an interesting piece of information: A well-known parable in Jesus' day was the story about Solomon and the missing *yod*. In Deuteronomy 17:16,17, God gives instructions to the king, *"You shall not multiply to yourself horses... wives."* Now, according to the story, the *yod* appeared before the throne of God and said, "Almighty, Solomon has thrown me out of his Scriptures." You see, when you remove the *yod*, from that particular text, it became "You shall multiply to yourself horses and wives." That's exactly what Solomon had done! He had thousands of horses in his stables and he had a thousand wives and concubines. According to the story, the missing *Yod*, caused Solomon not only to misinterpret, but literally to do exactly the opposite of what the Word said! So, the moral of the story was, for the lack of one small letter, the King was able to distort the Word of God!

So, Jesus was saying, "Not even the smallest letter will be destroyed or taken out." In other words, "I'm not going to let anyone destroy My Word or the meaning of My Word until everything is fulfilled."

---

34. Tverberg, Lois and Okkema, Bruce, *Listening to the Language of the Bible*, pp. 133-134.

Everyone listening, understood that expression because they were familiar with the story of the missing *Yod*.

BINDING AND LOOSING

In Matthew 16:19, the setting was at Caesarea Philippi, which is north of the Galilee. This was the place that Jesus often took His disciples. There were several reasons why He took them there. One of the main reasons was because this was under the rule of Philip the Tetrarch, who was the brother of Herod Antipas, the sons of Herod the Great. Herod Antipas was the one who had John the Baptist killed. Herod was the persecutor, and he even tried to arrest Jesus, but the Pharisees warned Him. In Luke 13:31, the Pharisees say, *"...depart from here, for Herod wants to kill You."* Jesus said, *"Tell that fox..."* So, Jesus took his disciples to a place where He wouldn't have to worry about Herod, plus there was no love lost between Philip and Herod. Do you know why? Check out Matthew 14:3,4.

At Caesarea Philippi, there was a large temple to the Greek god, Pan. Originally, it was called Paneas, Pan City, but it was changed to Baneas because the Arabs could not pronounce the letter 'P.' The ruins of the old temple were there, and also a huge cave, where one of the source waters of the Jordan river flowed out of. The cave was also called the gate, because that's where they thought the god Pan would go back and forth from hell to the upper world, through that gate. It was part of Mount Hermon; there was also a huge rock there. On that trip, Jesus used their surroundings to make His points. Geography has an input on the interpretation of this Scripture.

This was where Simon Peter made his wonderful declaration: According to Matthew 16:16, "*You are the Christ (Messiah), the Son of the living God.*" According to Luke 9:20, "*Meshiach-El,*" "*Messiah God.*" We translate it 'of God,' but it should be "God the *Messiah*." It's called *hendiadys,* a construct where two nouns are put together. Since there were few adjectives in Hebrew, they would put two nouns together and the second noun would describe the first.

"*You are God the Messiah*" or "*The Divine Messiah.*" Everyone was saying that Jesus was the *Messiah*, so if Peter had just said 'you are the Messiah,' it would have been no big deal. Peter's revelation was that <u>Jesus is God</u>! Jesus' response was, "*Blessed are you Simon Bar-Jonah, for flesh and blood have not revealed this to you, but My Father who is in heaven.*" Then He said, "*I will give you the keys of the Kingdom...*" Now, keys represent authority, but this is a special kind of authority. This has been discussed and debated down through the centuries. The Roman Catholic Church took one stand; the Protestant Church took another.

When does the householder turn his keys over to someone, and what kind of person does he turn them over to? In the time of Jesus, He would have been speaking of a steward! The steward was given responsibility and authority for the household and/or business. What was Joseph's position under Potiphar? In Genesis 39, it tells us he was Potiphar's overseer or steward. In other words, Potiphar gave Joseph authority over everything he had. Joseph was to buy and sell, as Potiphar would have done for himself. "*He left all he had in Joseph's hands."* The steward's job is to increase the master's property. In Matthew 25:14-30, that is why the wicked servant who buried the talent was condemned. Not just because he buried the talent, but because he knew what kind of person his master was, and he did not act accordingly. The steward was responsible to act with the master's property, in the master's best interest, the way the master would have done it himself.

Whenever Jesus said, *"I give you the keys to the kingdom,"* He was literally saying, I'm giving you authority and responsibility. You're going to act as my agent and therefore, whatever you decide, I'll back you up. Do you see what He is saying? The keys to the Kingdom is <u>stewardship authority</u>. If I'm acting as a steward, then I'm acting on God's behalf and all of my decisions will be to His glory. Therefore, whatever I do, when guided by God, He will back it up!

Do you see the whole idea of stewardship? This has ramifications for our whole lives and for our relationship with God! When we are acting as His steward, in good faith, His power and authority is there to back up what we say! So what did He say? (Matthew 16:19) *"Whatever you bind on earth will be bound in heaven"* by God! *"Whatever you loose on earth will be loosed in heaven."* He is handing authority to His servant! Now, we usually apply this to Spiritual Warfare, right? We think of binding the enemy. That is not what was meant here. That is not a wrong interpretation, but that's not what Jesus was saying to Peter here. Binding and loosing is another traditional, typical, Rabbinic term. We find it in the writings of the Rabbi. In fact, this was one of the major responsibilities of the Rabbi. It came down from the 70 Judges that God had Moses to appoint. It went down from the 70 Judges to the great Sanhedrin of the time of Ezra, down to the great Rabbis, like Hillel and Shammai. God had given them the right to make decisions on what was and was not permissible. That was what binding and loosing literally meant.[35]

Arnold Fruchtenbaum, a Messianic teacher, taught on binding and loosing using his great grandfather, who was a Rabbi in Poland, as his example. When tomatoes first came to their village, the people asked, "Rabbi, can we eat them or not, are they *Kosher*?" He studied the tomato, cut it open, examined the pieces according to the seed Law, examined the juice according to the juice Law, examined the meat and the color, then he made his decision. His decision was to loose them, he permitted them to eat the tomato. He was saying, 'It's Kosher, you are permitted, you are loosed, enjoy the tomato.' If he had bound it, he would have said, "No! No! No! You cannot eat it!"[36]

What was Jesus literally saying to Peter? "You have received revelation from God, so, I know you are in harmony with the Spirit of the LORD, thus I can entrust My following, My Kingdom into your hands. They are going to need to know what they can do and what they cannot do. With the leadership of the Holy Spirit, you will be able to guide them. Your word will be binding, because you are acting as My faithful steward."

Paul uses that in his first letter to the Corinthians, *"Am I not an Apostle?"* He goes on to suggest that the Apostles have the right to make decisions as to what is permissible and what is not permissible. He points out

---

35. Bivin, David, *Understanding the Difficult Words of Jesus,* pp. 105-109.
36. Fruchtenbaum, Arnold, *The Life of Jesus* (audio format).

that they are living in sin and that it is not permissible! That's what the whole letter is talking about. In the letter, he is binding certain activities and saying, "This is not permissible." He loosed them in other areas. He encourages them to do those things which <u>demonstrate the love of Christ</u>. Paul recognized that the authority that Jesus gave to Peter, went beyond Peter. It was truly the Apostolic role, because guidance had to be given to this new community of believers. Guidance on what was proper theology and proper behavior.

Now, how does this relate to <u>*Spiritual Warfare*</u>? I believe that every believer has the authority, if they are acting under His leadership, as God's steward. That's the key, we have to be under His authority, and we have to be in a proper relationship and obedient to His will for the binding and loosing to be effective. God is not obligated to fulfill something that we speak out of our own desire, apart from His will. We do not have the authority on our own to bind anything, it is only through the name and power of Jesus. When we bind a spirit in Jesus' name, we are forbidding that spirit to act out or to operate in our lives.

What happens too often is, we bind with our words and loose with our actions! We proclaim wonderful declarations, "I bind you, Satan!" In the first place, we can't bind Satan! After the fall, he was given permission by God, actually by man's actions! When we do things in our lives, in terms of sin, those sins give the enemy every legal right to do whatever he wants! If we pick up the enemy's tools, we need to realize the enemy comes with them. What are some of the enemy's tools? An easy tool of the enemy for Christians to pick up is the critical nature, actually we should call it a critical spirit.

Gossip is also an easy one, but look at Mark 7:21,22 for a good list.

Technically, binding and loosing means: forbid and permit. In Spiritual Warfare, we are telling the enemy, "I forbid you to be a part of my life, in Jesus' name!" Then comes the hard part, <u>walking it out</u>, not permitting the enemy back in. Spiritual Warfare doesn't end with the proclamation of freedom from the enemy, we have to live in that freedom every day.

Anything that we bind or loose has to be totally in line with God's will. This will be dealt with in more depth, when we delve into 'The Kingdom of God'. Remember what the Centurion said in Matthew 8:8,9, *"...only speak the word...for I also am a man under authority..."* He understood the authority that Jesus was under. That's the key! If Jesus was under authority, He had authority and God backed up what He said and did. <u>He did what He saw His Father do</u>.

That's why Jesus said, *"If you have faith, and you speak it in faith...."* it will be done. If we speak in faith, we are putting ourselves under and submitting to God's authority and He will be there to back up our words. It is never our authority; it is always <u>God's authority</u>. Staying under God's authority is the hard part, but that is a requirement! <u>Under His authority, All Things are Possible</u>!

Isaiah 51, says, *"Look to the rock from which you were hewn and the hole of the pit from which you were dug. Look to Abraham your father and to Sarah who bore you."* The Jewish teaching on that is: 'When God looked down through time and He saw how bad man was going to get,' He said, 'How can I bring Myself to create this being,' but when He looked a little further and saw

Abraham, He said, 'There is the rock on whom I can build."

In Matthew 16:18, "...*on this rock,*" represents four things:

1. Jesus implies the same thing: "Peter, I can see beyond you. I see through the weaknesses. You are the rock I can build on."

2. Peter had just received Divine Revelation, in other words, he was in communion with the Holy Spirit because God was giving him direct revelation. That was what Jesus was going to build on, on revelation, on communion with God!

3. Jesus was saying, 'Now that I see you're receiving revelation from God, this is the rock that I can build on. The Church will make the declaration, Jesus is Lord!'

4. Jesus Himself is the Rock on which He builds His Church! He was implying, Peter, which means a 'little piece of the rock,' you are a big part of this, but I will build on the Boulder. *Petra* means 'the Boulder,' "**I will build My Church**!" I'm going to build a Church on Me. We don't know if He gestured to Himself. He could have meant any of those four. It could be Himself, or Peter the man, or the act of getting the revelation, or the revelation itself, and it really may be a combination of all of these. He said, "I will build My Church, on My Covenant Communion, My Family, My Witnessing Community." He also declared ownership... "*I* will build *My*...." It is sad to say, but this is the part that too many churches ignore!

CIRCUMLOCUTION

I hate listening to a teacher that when they finish, you sit there and think, "That sounded great, but I didn't understand a word of it!" To me the gift of teaching should be putting truths, Divine Mystery into understandable language so that people can walk away and say, "Oh, That's what it means." That is the real goal of teaching. Teaching is not about impressing people with one's knowledge, or using big words that the students don't understand. If the teacher doesn't make it understandable, what has the teacher accomplished? God wants His Word understood, not just proclaimed!

After saying that, I want to share one of those big words, circumlocution. But, it is a very important concept to understand in our Jewish Roots studies. Circumlocution is a nice big word that means something very simple; *circum* means 'around,' *locution* means 'a word, phrase, or expression,' so circumlocution means, 'to talk around.' Let me explain. In Exodus 20:7, God gave a Command, *"You shall not take the name of the LORD your God in vain."* What that means is, you should not use the name of the LORD your God in an unholy way, because how you use a name, or how you deal with the name of a person is how you deal with that person. In the Hebrew understanding, the name cannot be separated from the identity of the person. They believed that the name stamped that person with the character identity. In Geneses 35:17, Rachel was dying giving birth, she called out the baby's name *"Ben-Oni,"* which means "son of my sorrows." Jacob rejected that name, and named him *Benjamin* which means "son of my right hand." When God allowed Adam to name all the animals, He was allowing him to be part of the creative process. God brought the animals to him, and Adam was participating by stamping the character or nature on them when he named them.

So, if we use God's name in a way that's less than Holy, we're saying that God is less than Holy! God was saying, "Do not use My name in a way that is less than Holy." God gave His name to Moses, "*YHWH*," which has a breathy sound. Then He said in Exodus 3:14, 'You tell the people that this is My name. "*I Am who I Am.*" In other words, 'I will be who I will be, I was who I was, I will do what I will do, I am *YHWH*.' So Moses gives this name to the Hebrews and it's used for a period of time. After a while, they became afraid that they might use it in a way that was less than Holy. By the Second Temple period, they had stopped using the name of God and started substituting other words. Then they even stopped using the word 'God' and began substituting other words for that as well.[37] Circumlocution is simply a substitution for God's Name in the text. Rather than saying the word 'God' or *YHWH*, they substituted other words. We find this very often, "*Blessed are the poor in spirit for theirs is the kingdom of heaven.*" This is a perfect example of circumlocution!

In Luke, we do not find the Kingdom of heaven, He only used Kingdom of God. Why? Luke's writings were primarily to the Gentiles. They were not offended by the use of the word God, so Luke was free to use it. Matthew, being very Hebraic, used 'The Kingdom of heaven.' In fact, the only mention of Kingdom of heaven in the entire New Testament is found in Matthew.

---

37. Bivin, David, *Understanding the Difficult Words of Jesus*, p. 59.

Kingdom of heaven was a Jewish way of saying 'Kingdom of God.' Heaven is a circumlocution for God,[38] so as to not break the Third Commandment.

Have you heard people teach that 'the Kingdom of God and the Kingdom of heaven' are different, that one refers to an earthly Kingdom and the other refers to where we go when we die? Kingdom of heaven and Kingdom of God are exactly the same thing! It's just that one is very Greek and the other is a very Hebraic way of using a substitution for the name of God. They used circumlocution to read around God's name, so what did they substitute? They substituted the word *'Adonai.' Adonai* means 'LORD.' The LORD of Lords is GOD! If you are ever in a Messianic or Jewish service, you will not hear, *Baruch atah Yah-weh,* you will hear *Baruch atah Adonai.* They substitute the word *'Adonai'* in their prayers and Scriptures.

Adonai brings me to a point that I need to discuss. It is the common name that has been given to God, the name Jehovah. You will not find this word in the Hebrew Scriptures. It comes from circumlocution! God's name is <u>YHWH</u>. It's called a *Tetragrammaton,* which means four letters, and this is the <u>Holy Name of God</u>. Early Hebrew had no vowels, only consonants, and the vowels were understood. There were 22 letters in the alphabet. *Yah weh* [yaa wày] is the best we know how to pronounce it, because we don't know for sure how it was pronounced. Why? Because they quit pronouncing God's name! The only time it was ever pronounced was on the Day of Atonement by the High Priest, and that ended when the Temple was destroyed

---

38. Flusser, David, *Jesus*, p. 105.

in 70 AD. Whenever you see the words 'I AM" in scripture, it is YHWH, *Yah weh*, God's Holy name.

When they developed the *Masoretic* Formula, which are vowels, they said, "How are we going to remind people not to read *Yah weh*, but to read *Adonai* whenever they see *Yah-weh* in the Scriptures. They did not want anyone to slip and read *Yah weh*, because they didn't want them to sin by using it in an unholy way. So what did they do? They put the vowels of *Adonai* above the word YHWH, so the reader had the consonants of YHWH with the vowels of *Adonai* above.

When the English translators came along, not knowing what the Scribes had done, they combined the consonants YHWH and the vowels of Adonai, thus they ended up with Yehowah. The W and the V are interchangeable, and so is the Y and the J. The early translators, who were German, were more prone to this interchangeability, thus this eventually became Jehovah! They combined the two, so actually the word Jehovah is a combination of the word *'Yah-weh'* and the word *'Adonai.'* It is a *syncretistic* word, where two words are combined and brought together to form one word. God is not offended if someone uses "Jehovah," but I want you to know that technically it is not His name, it is either *Adonai* or *Yah weh*. Out of respect for our Jewish brothers, we do not use *Yah weh*. This is very offensive to a believing Jew, and even some in the Messianic community. They will write 'G-d' or 'L-RD,' out of respect, not wanting to use it in an unholy way.

What did God mean when He said, *"Do not take my name in vain?"* He does not want His name used in less than a Holy way, because it tells the world that we consider Him less than Holy. When I hear people say,

"By God," "Oh my God," or "Jesus Christ," I just cringe! I'm sorry, but they are using it as an expletive, actually, a slang word, and that is not in a Holy way! They are declaring to the world that their opinion of God is not very high. I know it becomes a habit, but that's a habit that needs to be broken.

By the way, did you know that you carry the name of God on you? In Revelation 9:4 He said, *"the seal of God on their forehead."* And 14:1 says, *"having the Father's name written on their foreheads."* If God's name is written on us spiritually, it should affect how we live our lives! We carry the Name, the seal of God on us, so what we do every day either honors His Holy Name or takes His name in vain. This is what God was saying in the third commandment, Exodus 20:7, *"Thou shalt not take the name of the LORD thy God in vain,"* which means, if I'm a Holy person, I'm honoring God and His Holiness.

Jesus was not going to use the Name of the LORD in a way that was less than Holy, but He uses circumlocution. Why? He did it because He did not want to offend the people He was sent to. We find a perfect example of this at Jesus' trial, He was standing before the High Priest. The High Priest asked Him, *"Are you the Messiah?"* Remember Christ is the Greek word for the Hebrew word Messiah, they are the same word. In Luke 22:68-70, Jesus said, *"If I tell you, you would not believe Me. If I ask you, you will not answer Me. But I tell you this: I see the Son of Man sitting at the right hand of the Power...!"* Then the High Priest said, *"Then you are claiming to be the Son of the Blessing!"* The Priest tore his robe, which by the way, broke Jewish Law. The High Priest was not allowed to tear his garment! He yelled

"*Blasphemy,*" and sentenced Jesus to death. Legally, they couldn't put Jesus' to death, so they had the Romans carry out His execution.

What is Jesus saying here? "I saw the Son of Man." This is His favorite term for Himself. He answered them in Matthew 26:64, "*Sitting at the right hand of the Power!*" What's the Power? It is a circumlocution for the name of God! Now when the Son is sitting at the right hand of the Father, what does that remind you of? It is found in Psalm 110, "*Sit at My right hand till I make Your enemies Your footstool.*" "*The LORD said to my Lord....*" What Jesus was saying is, "You're judging me now, but ultimately I'm going to be your Judge." He told them in a Jewish way who He was and they shouted, "*Blasphemer.*" He used the term Power. He didn't say "the right hand of God." He said, "The right hand of the Power," and they knew exactly what He was saying.

Another circumlocution we have already been using, but have not identified as such, is *HaShem,* which is literally the Name! Many Orthodox Jews will refer to God as "*HaShem,*" Blessed be the Name. We find circumlocutions all through the Scriptures. Don't let this confuse you when reading the Scriptures. This just shows us how Hebraic the Scriptures are.

CHAPTER FIVE
TOOLS THAT JESUS USED

PARABLES

Jesus used the Rabbinical techniques of the parable to get His message across to the people. The use of parables was probably the most common Rabbinic teaching method of that day. So you see, parables did not originate with Jesus, He adopted the methods of the culture that He was in. When parables were used, they were always told in pairs to make a point. Examples in Jesus' teaching would be, "the pearl of great price and the field with the treasure."[39] Another example would be, "the lost coin and the lost sheep."[40] Sadly to say, many of Jesus' parables have been separated or else the second one was lost. The Jerusalem School of Synoptic Studies are attempting to find the pairs that have been separated in Scripture and bring them back together again.

I've heard it said that Jesus taught openly until He reached a point, then, from that point on, He taught in parables so the people wouldn't understand and only a select few would understand the Word. That is so very incorrect! The whole purpose of a parable was, like a sermon illustration, to make the point so that people could see it and grasp the meaning. He was putting it in a common setting, a situation that related to their lives, so people could understand. Now, occasionally His parables could be very allegorical. The Parable of the

---

39. Hayford, Jack (General Editor), Nelson's New King James, *Matthew* 13:44-46.
40. Ibid, *Luke* 15:1-10.

Sower is almost an allegory.

In the Prodigal Son, or The Loving Father as I like to call it, the meaning is very obvious. The father that loved the son so much, he never turned against him, and when the son comes back, he embraces him and welcomes him home. Jesus is talking about God here and it was very obvious to those that were listening to Him. They knew exactly what He was talking about.

Many of the parables seem vague or difficult to understand, but remember we are looking back nearly two thousand years into a very foreign culture. That is why studies like this are so important. When we look at the Parable of the Sower, we have to dig deep. The meanings are not as obvious. In Matthew 13:1-23, the disciples are confused about its meaning. Jesus was saying, "*You've been given the Mysteries of the Kingdom,*" of all people, you should understand this! We also find, "*...hear and they do not hear...see and they do not see, and they don't understand.*" Jesus quoted from Isaiah 6:9,10.

Basically, what God was saying in Isaiah is, "I am sending you to a stiff-necked people. They will hear your words, but they will not understand or turn from their evil ways." Was this God's desire for His people? No, by no means, He wants all mankind to turn to Him. We could say that God was warning Isaiah that "in spite of what I desire for them, most will not hear. The job I am giving you will not be easy, in fact you will be rejected, and ultimately, it will cost you your life."

Jesus was not trying to be secretive. This was not meant to be only understood by His chosen few, His disciples. But, He knew for some, it would be too deep. Basically Jesus was saying, "They just don't get it. I want to forgive them, I want them to understand it, but they will not seek to understand." Paul would have said something like, "They want to be fed baby's milk, not meat." After all, didn't Jesus come "*to seek and save the lost*," Luke 19:10. He came to show us God's love, and mature the Bride.

We have to remember, all we have is the raw words, and they can be misleading if we don't catch the point. So, understand that sometimes there will be scripture that looks like they're contradictory to the nature of God. In those cases, you have to say, 'Is this His nature.' <u>I truly encourage you to pray when dealing with those difficult scriptures. Let the Holy Spirit show you His truth!</u>

Parables were not meant to be obscure in their meaning, they were designed to make a point, to illuminate! We have parables throughout all the literature of the *Talmud* and the Jewish writings throughout the ages. Usually they begin with, "With what should I compare this?" or "How can I compare this?" With Jesus, we don't have those statements. Why? He either didn't use that phrase, or the writers didn't feel it was important that it be included. They may have felt that the parable itself was all that was important. Jesus would often begin his parable with, "*There was a certain man....*"

Were Jesus' parables true? They may have been true, we really don't know. Some good sermon illustrations are based on truth, from real life experiences, while others may have a kernel of truth in them, or they may be purely fictional. They are used as illustrations to make a point, to show the meaning. We consider this perfectly legitimate, and that is exactly what a parable was. Jesus used parables extensively and the whole purpose was to make things plain! The parables were phrased in the language and experiences that the people of that day could understand.

In Matthew 13, Jesus begins, *"Behold, a sower went out to sow?"* When we are going to sow a crop, we don't just throw the seeds everywhere? Things are different in Israel. In order to get a crop, some ground can be plowed, but most of it can't, because of the rocky soil! It is the rockiest land I have ever seen, there are rocks everywhere! It is hard ground, so they have to make it yield. So, the sower would go out and he would sow by hand. He couldn't even bring his animals through parts of it, thus he sowed by hand and he harvested by hand.

You see, they understood that the sower would broadcast the seed and some would fall on the rocks, some would fall on the hard paths where people walked, some would fall among the thorns and weeds, but some would fall on good ground. This does not fit the American style of agriculture for growing a good crop. We clear the land and cultivate it, then plant it, but there, they could not do that, so the sower going out to sow makes perfect sense to the listeners.

The parables were given so that they would understand what He was saying. If Jesus had come today, parables would include modern transportation and manufacturing. The whole point was to make it plain to the people He was sent to. We use illustrations and stories, because they are remembered. A teaching may be forgotten, but a parable sticks in a person's mind.

PARABLES: THE PRODIGAL SON

Parables basically had a goal; they almost always ended unfinished! In the Prodigal Son for example, does the older brother go in? We don't know, it stops! Why? Because the parables were designed to make the listener make a decision: "Who am I in the story?" and "What would I do?" "Am I more like the loving father, the prodigal son, or the older brother? I am sure Jesus was an awesome story teller, and His audience hung on every word. Jesus wanted His audience to grapple with their own lives, their situations, and draw nearer to God. The word prodigal means wasteful. The prodigal was obviously the sinner, coming back to the LORD. The older brother was the people that were trying to live righteous lives. The question was and still is, "What are you going to do?" It is left up to the listener, we are forced to make a decision.

Parables were also known for their shock value. The Parable of the Prodigal Son is filled with things that contradict their social expectations. For example, when the younger son goes and asks for his inheritance, understand, that was never done in Jewish society! Children never have the right to ask for their inheritance early. The father could give it early if he wanted to, but asking for the inheritance was unheard of. In fact, there is only one instance that we have in the Talmud of a son asking his father for his inheritance early, and the father died six months later. The wife swore he died of a broken heart because he had been so disgraced by his son. You see, if the inheritance is asked for early, it is like saying, "I wish you were dead! I want all that's coming to me when you die, and I want it now!" The prodigal son disgraces his father over and over again. He flaunts his rebellion against his father in the face of everyone. That's the theme of this story.

God, the loving Father, was being slapped in the face by the children He loves so much, and when they choose to return to Him, how does He respond? He runs to meet them, wraps His arms around them, hugs them, and welcomes them home! That's the love of the Father! That's the theme of this parable, but every step along the way was shocking to the listeners. Even the father running was shocking! Jewish men of that day did not run, they walked with dignity! When the father ran, he had to take his robes and tuck them into his girdle, baring his legs. Everyone lived in villages for safety and went out to their fields. In front of all of his neighbors, who were watching, because they had heard the son was coming home, he disgraced himself for the love of his son!

Now, what does that say about God? He sent His Son to die on the cross! That was the most disgraceful way to die! Jesus hung there fully naked, so very humiliating, especially for a Jewish man of that day. God doesn't care if that was a disgrace, if that was what was required, Jesus does it willingly. He meets His children with open arms, upon their return.

Do you see His tremendous love? Everyone listening to that story was shocked beyond belief at the way the father acted. The purpose of Jesus' shocking them was to make them think, 'That is what God is like.' You see, it had impact. Parables were designed to impact people's lives, to overwhelm them! They would not forget that story! That's the purpose of a parable. Today you will hear the world refer to the Prodigal Son.

See, it stuck! That's the purpose of a parable.

What was the worst thing a Jew could end up doing? Working on a pig farm, that was the lowest of low. Understand, the pig is the most despicable animal on earth to a Jew! Why? Because in the Jewish *Kosher* Laws, any animal can be eaten that has a split hoof and chews the cud. A pig has a split hoof, but it does not chew the cud. It is the chief of the hypocrites because it appears clean on the outside, but it is not because it does not fulfill the Law. The pig was symbolic in Jewish thinking as the lowest form of animal. Therefore, the idea of taking care of pigs in the parable was Jesus' way of showing His listeners just how bad things had gotten! The son had reached the very bottom! In fact, since we know pigs are being raised, this tells us he had left the land of Israel. He was in a pagan country. You see, he was even running from God. That's part of the story that is hidden from us, if we don't read our Scripture closely or understand the culture.

I have heard people say, "What Jesus taught is not important. All that matters is after the crucifixion." My favorite word for them is, "ba-lon-ey!" Why? Because, if Jesus is the Word of God made flesh, when Jesus speaks, God is speaking, and if God is speaking, I want to know what He is saying. In my opinion, we had better listen! Jesus' teachings are as important as what He did on the cross!

Jesus did not come to die on the cross or to be raised from the dead! Those were the tools God used, the way God accomplished His purpose. The reason Jesus came was to restore the relationship that was broken in the Garden of Eden. Now, how was He going to do that? He did it by dying! He did it through the resurrection! The death and the resurrection were a necessity, but He did not come just to die, He came to restore the relationship! Relationship is the whole theme of His teachings!

The parables are geared toward restoring a proper relationship in life, so His parables are going to emphasize that. If He came to restore relationship, why would He want to obscure the message from the very people He was trying to reach? See, it does not make sense to think He was obscuring His message. That kind of thinking has even infiltrated the Church of today. This is an error that needs to be corrected! Jesus used Scripture, illustrations, and interpretations to show what the Scripture is all about. He used parables to illustrate His point, and He was always teaching out of love. When we learn to look through the eyes and experiences of the First Century Jew, we will see that.

LIGHT AND HEAVY

The Rabbis had a whole listing of specific Rabbinical teaching techniques and Jesus used them. One of them was known as 'from light to heavy.' In other words, if the light thing is true, how much more will the heavy thing be true? An example of this is found in Matthew 7:11, "*If you then, being evil, know how to give good gifts to your children, how much more will your heavenly Father give...?*" This is *kal va-homer*, from light to heavy.[41] "*If you, being evil...,*" does not mean you are evil, it means you are not as good as God. We have a sinful nature. Do you see it, from light to heavy? *Kal va-homer* is saying 'if you can't do the light thing, what makes you think you're going to be able to do the heavy thing. Once, in my ministry, I was having what I considered a major difficulty with a certain person on the session. I was praying about the problem and God spoke to me. He said "If you can't handle this small thing, how do you expect to handle the big things." This is a perfect example of *kal va-homer*, at my expense.

Kal va-homer can be used in a positive way or a negative way. The Rabbis moved from the light to the heavy all the time. There is also a sense of progression in terms of evil, or mistakes. People do not just jump into heavy sins, they go from a small sin, which leads to a heavier sin, which leads to a greater sin. That is the whole issue, for example, of murder. In Matthew 5:21-22, Jesus said, "*You have heard it said... 'You shall not murder'...but I say to you, whoever is angry with his brother without a cause shall be in danger of the judgment.*" Basically, what He meant by this is, if you have a problem with your brother and you don't seek to resolve it, he could take you to the local Court! They would bring it to the court and say something like, "Here is my brother who refuses to seek peace and harmony with me." Now, the Court of that community could find for one or the other. They could take property away or hand out punishment. They could give out stripes or lashes! They could give out up to Thirty-nine lashes! Forty was

---

41. Tverberg, Lois and Okkema, Bruce, *Listening to the Language of the Bible*, pp. 131-132.

the maximum number of lashes, but they never gave more than thirty-nine. Do you know why? What if they lost count and miscounted by one? They would be breaking the Law! So they always gave one less than the Law allowed. That way if they miscounted, they wouldn't go over what the Law required.

'If there is anger between you and your brother, and you don't resolve it, you can be taken to court.' Then He said, "*Whoever says to your brother, raca, shall be in danger of the council.*" They could really be called before the Council. Why? "*Raca*" is a Jewish word that coincides with our word "airhead," it was slander! Remember, in the Jewish way of thinking, what was done to the name, was done to the person. To treat the name with disrespect is disrespecting the person and that is slander! Slander was one of the big offenses of that day. The punishment for slander could've been imprisonment for a period of time, or they could've been fined heavily! In other words, it is a heavy word for being angry. Angry is the light one, the next, a little heavier, and the next, if you say, "*You fool, you're in danger of the judgment, Hell fire!*"

Whoa! What does He mean? To us saying, "You fool" is the same thing as calling someone an airhead. Obviously, that is not what it meant to the Jews of the First Century. Psalm 14:1 tells us what a fool is, "*The fool says in his heart, there is no God.*" No one was an atheist in those days, everyone believed in some form of god(s). So what is he saying? 'The fool says in his heart, I don't care whether there is a God or not, I'll do what I want to do! God isn't going to judge me. I'm free to do whatever I want to do.' He's a total reprobate! In other words, he has totally turned his back on God. He's not really a nonbeliever, he just doesn't believe that God is going to do anything to him. So, in Jesus' time, if someone said, "You fool," they were basically saying, "You're going to Hell!" Do you see the light to heavy?

Matthew 7:1,2 says, *"Judge not, that you be not judged. For with what judgment you judge, and with the measure you use, it will be measured back to you."* So, if we judge our brother, "You're going to Hell! I judge you as a reprobate." We have just judged ourselves. Why? Because that's something that only God can say. We don't know what's going on in that person's heart, we don't know how God is dealing with that person. That's why Jesus said, "Don't judge!"

This doesn't mean that we shouldn't make decisions about what is right behavior and what is wrong behavior, or even judge the character of a person. That is not what Jesus is saying here. What He means is that we are not in a position to pass eternal judgment on anyone. We don't know what God is going to do in that person's life. It is like someone dies and people say, "Well, we know where he went." My wife's grandmother quoted an old saying: "We don't know what decision was made between the saddle and the ground." We cannot know what happened in the last few minutes of a person's life. All we can say is that we know what God expects and we don't see the fruit in that person's life. It is God's call, not ours.

In the teaching on "you fool," Jesus is not saying that you're actually going to send yourself to Hell, He is saying, "Don't you see what you're doing? You're speaking a curse over yourself when you speak a curse on someone else. You're actually cursing yourself, for you'll get back what you give."

To use one of Barney Fife's (the deputy on the Andy Griffith T.V. show) favorite sayings, and it fits beautifully here, "Nip it in the bud!" It is easier to stop anger then to let it build to slander, and then build to judging and condemnation. What is the next step? Murder! All these are lighter forms of murder. It is a simple set of steps to go from telling someone to go to Hell and actually trying to send them there. Jesus is saying that murder can be more than just taking the life. It is in the attitude that we have toward our brother. That is the light and the heavy. *"If they persecute Me… how much more will they persecute you,"* John 15:20. 'If they blaspheme Me, how much more will they blaspheme you?' How many times do we see Jesus using those expressions? 'How much more' is a way of saying light to heavy?

Do you see the progression? There is an old Jewish saying: "it's much easier to pull up a sapling than it is to pull up a full grown oak tree." When the oak tree first starts coming up out of an acorn, it's easy to pull it up. But, if we let it grow, it becomes difficult, if not impossible, to pull up. If we catch it while it's in the bud, the beginning stages, it's much easier to stop. That's the whole principle of light to heavy. When Jesus was talking about a negative, if the light is true and you don't stop it, it will become heavy.

The word murder in Hebrew is *ratzach*, and the word kill is *hatag*. In Hebrew, there is a totally different distinction between the two.[42] The word *ratzach* was used in the Ten Commandments. *Ratzach* means to take a life in a premeditated way. It did not apply murder to

---

42. Bivin, David, *Understanding the Difficult Words of Jesus*, p. 69.

the killing of animals, protecting one's life, or to warfare. These acts were never conceivable by the Jewish people as being *ratzach*. Warfare and self-defense were totally different matters. The Jewish attitude was, if you knew someone was on his way to your house to kill you, you had the right to rise up earlier and kill him first! Why? Because life is to be protected. Life is God's greatest gift. That's why if the ox is in the ditch on the Sabbath, you can get it out! Why? Life is to be protected! The march around Jericho lasted seven days, right? One of those days had to have been on *Shabbat*, but they marched anyway! They broke the Law. Why? God had given them a <u>command</u>, and that takes precedence over everything. You do God's command! You do what is necessary to preserve life! You do what is necessary to do God's will!

MEASURE FOR MEASURE

The next Rabbinical teaching technique that I want us to look at is called, "Measure for measure." Measure for measure is whatever was given out, that's what is gotten back, or what you sow, you reap. This is the theme over and over in Jesus' teachings. 'If this is true then the equal will be true. If you bless, then you will be blessed. If you curse, you will be cursed. If you give, you will receive. If you hoard, you will lose.' *"So what does it profit a man, if he gains the whole world and loses his soul,"* Matthew 16:26. The measure of losing life to God is gaining life from God! We get what we give, measure for measure. We are going to reap what we sow; if we give love, we are going to reap love.

Eye for an eye was a perfect example of measure for measure. Understand that "eye for an eye" does not mean that if a victim's eye was knocked out, he has the right to take out the guilty party's eye. In fact, "eye for an eye" was the lowest form of punishment handed down by the courts. It was actually meant as a limitation on punishment, not for revenge. In other words, the most that could be done to the guilty party would be equivalent to what they had done. It could be anything less than, but it could not exceed that point, and it did not include maiming the guilty party's body. The council was responsible for handing down the punishment, not the individual. Individual vengeance was never allowed.

That brings us to the story of the unjust or dishonest servant, as he was called in Luke 16:1-13. Someone accuses the steward of wasting the master's goods. The master told the steward that he was going to fire him. He had accounts payable that hadn't been paid. The steward is responsible for collecting the debt, which was one of the main parts of his job. The master had been loaning commodities, or money, and the loans hadn't been repaid. So the steward went to the debtor and said, 'Look, you owe a hundred measures of oil, tear up that bill and write it out for fifty. To another, he changed it to eighty from one hundred measures of wheat.' It looks like he was cheating his master. I wonder if he was canceling out the interest owed, plus giving up his own commission. Out of the whole thing, the master got back what he had loaned and the people that owed the debt paid less than they would have had to pay. The master praises the servant for his shrewd dealings. So what happened? The steward made friends of the master and the debtors. He states that he didn't want to beg and couldn't do any other kind of job. He knew that if the master fired him, he could go to those people that he helped. That's the whole point of the parable, measure for measure. He gave out mercy in hopes that he would be able to receive mercy.

What about the man that was given mercy and didn't return mercy? In Matthew 18:23-35, the king forgave a debt that the man could never have paid off in his lifetime. Then the forgiven man went out to a man who owed him a very small debt, like $50, and had that man thrown into prison because he couldn't pay the debt. The king heard what the man he forgave had done and the king, taking back the forgiveness, threw the wicked servant into prison, until the debt was paid in full! Mercy was given, but mercy was not shown. What he received, he did not give.

REMEZ

The third technique that we're going to look at is *Remez*, which means to allude to. In Luke 23:28-31, Jesus was on the way to the cross. The women of Jerusalem see Jesus and begin to weep. Why were they crying? Because they realize that their Messiah was going to be crucified. Jesus said, *"Daughters of Jerusalem, don't weep for Me. Weep for yourselves... For if they do these things in the green wood, what will be done in the dry?"* What does He mean? It makes no sense to us whatsoever, right? This is *Remez*! Anytime you run into a passage of Jesus' teachings that seems to make no sense, stop and dig. Remember, Jesus quoted Scripture all the time. What Scripture did He quote? The Old Testament, so, use the concordance to look up "green wood or green tree." Remember, don't just read the verse, read the chapter, or chapters, surrounding it. The concordance will lead you to Ezekiel 20:47b,48. Let's back up to verse 45, and read through 21:7. God was passing judgment on the people and Ezekiel was saying that the wrath of God was like a fire that would burn up and destroy even the green tree.

Let me demonstrate what the rabbinical process would have been like. This Scripture made the Rabbi's question, 'What was God talking about, a destructive fire that would destroy even the green tree? Green versus dry, dry is obviously dead, green is alive! One with life and the other death. Obviously the one that has life is righteous, Holy! The one that's dead would be the one without life. So, who or what would be the Holy Tree? Their conclusion was, it was the Messiah! The coming Messiah will be the Green Tree!' So "Green Tree," became the code-word for Messiah. He is the one who will be the bearer of life. So everyone else is going to be what? A dry tree! So what was Jesus saying here? 'If they do this to Me, the Messiah, what will they do to you?' Do you see the light and the heavy in this?

As He prophesied here, 40 years later, Jerusalem was destroyed. The people were starved, and the ones that tried to flee the city were crucified by the Romans inside the city walls. It was a time of slaughter, a horrid time in Jewish history. Titus came in with the Roman army and destroyed Jerusalem. The Zealots were the ones that sealed up the walls and forced the people to stay in the city, they didn't want anyone to escape. In fact, a most distinguished disciple of Rabbi Hillel, Rabbi Jochanan ben Zakkai, was in the city and knew the destruction was coming. The Zealots were guarding the gates and they wouldn't let anyone out. So, Rabbi ben Zakkai got into a coffin and pretended to be dead, and his Disciples carried him out. This was very dangerous, because every time anyone brought a coffin out, the Zealots would run their sword through the coffin to make sure the person was dead! Jochanan ben Zakkai was a great teacher, and was well respected by the people. Because of this, the Zealots would not defile his body by running it through, a response that Rabbi ben Zakkai was counting on. He escaped from Jerusalem and the Romans let them go because they didn't want anything to do with a burial. He and his disciples went to the city of Jabneh where later on, after the Roman period, he re-establishes the Sanhedrin. This became the post-destruction Sanhedrin that eventually moved to Tiberius and continued to make decisions that affected Jewish history from 90 AD and on.[43]

    Jesus was warning the women of the terrible destruction that was to come in 40 short years. He spoke prophetically by using *Remez*, 'The Green Tree.' He was proclaiming Himself to be the Messiah on His way to the crucifixion. Those that heard Him, knew exactly what He was saying. He was saying, "<u>I am the Messiah!</u>"

    Another example of *remez* is found in Matthew 24:28, the Disciples are asking, *"Tell us, when will these things be? And what will be the sign of Your coming and the end of the age?"* Those were their questions, three

---

43. Cohen, Abraham, *Everyman's Talmud*, pp. .xli-xliii.

separate questions. In Matthew 24:4-51 and Mark 13:5-27, Jesus' answers are not separated. If we use the passage from Luke 21:8-28, he breaks down the answers a little better. When Jesus came to the end of His answer, He said in Matthew 24: 27, *"When they say the Messiah is here or the Messiah is there, don't go."* Then He said, *"The lightning flashes from the east to the west, so will the coming of the Son of Man be."* In other words, it is going to happen instantaneously. When we see the storm, we don't know when or where the lightning is going to strike, we can't predict it. We get a sense of the signs of the times, but we don't know the exact time. When lightning flashes, everyone sees it, it's known. There are different ways this can be understood.

Jesus said in verse 28, *"For wherever the carcass is, there the eagles will be gathered together."* Now some translations say vultures, but it is not vultures, it is eagles! When eagles migrate and they come into areas where other eagles live, the newcomers will become scavengers. They are normally hunters, but they won't compete for the food source with the local eagles, so they scavenge on the dead carcasses.

Jesus said, '...where the dead body is...' So, what does He mean? Here's a reference, Job 39:27-30. Let me paraphrase this text. God is talking to Job after he said, 'I've had enough of this, and I'm going to confront God!' God answers Job, "...where were you when I created the heavenly bodies and the earth? Does the hawk fly at your command? Did you tell him how to hunt? What about the eagle? The eagle builds his nest high. Did you show him how? An eagle builds his nest and his brood never lack for food. For where the slain are, that's where the eagles will be." In other words, the eagle knows how to hunt on his own. You didn't teach it. Who teaches the eagle to hunt? God does! So, what was Jesus saying here?

There are several interpretations of this; I have mine. David Bivin has a slightly different interpretation. David doesn't say I'm wrong, he thinks that what Jesus was saying was that when it happens, it happens. When Jesus comes back, we'll know it! Now, that's one way of looking at it.

The way I see this is, "Who tells the eagle how to hunt? God does." So, who's in charge, when all of this will happen? God's in charge! I back up my theory with Acts 1:7, after the resurrection; Jesus said, "*It is not for you to know times or seasons, which the Father has put in His own authority.*" God's going to decide when. I believe these passages are tied together. I believe Jesus was saying, 'you're asking Me when, the answer is, not even the Son knows when,' only the Father knows. It's under His authority, and it's going to happen when God decides it's time for it to happen. God is the one who is in charge of this, the will of the Father. This is *remez*, and also in Job. So, when you run into one of those difficult passages, it should be a red flag, a place to dig for the hidden treasures.

CHAPTER SIX
JESUS' FAVORITE TOOL

NATHANAEL

This is truly one of my favorite examples of the discoveries available through the Jewish Roots study. In John 1:43-51, Jesus had just called Philip to be one of His Disciples. Philip runs to a man named Nathanael and said, *"We have found Him of whom Moses in the law, and also the prophets wrote, Jesus of Nazareth, the son of Joseph."* Now, Nathanael knew his Scriptures and said, *"Can anything good come out of Nazareth!"* In other words, how can the <u>Good One</u> come out of Nazareth? You see, Nazareth was a small hillside community in Galilee and it did not hold significance in Scriptures concerning the Messiah. Nathanael knew 'The Good One was going to come out of Bethlehem.' He was asking a serious theological question. What did Philip say to him? *"Come and see."* In other words, 'If you have trouble believing what I say, fine! Come and check it out for yourself.'

So, here comes Nathanael, walking toward Jesus. Jesus said, *"Behold, an Israelite indeed, in whom is no guile,"* meaning no deceit. Nathanael said, *"How do You know me?"* Jesus answers, *"Before Philip called you, when you were sitting under the fig tree, I saw you."* Now, look at Nathanael's response: *"You are the Son of God! You are the King of Israel!"* In other words, You're the Messiah! Excuse me? All Jesus said was, *"I saw you sitting under the fig tree before Philip called you,"* and Nathanael's response is, 'You've got to be the Messiah!' Obviously something is going on here that is not really understood in our way of thinking. We need to look at the customs, the expectations, and the teaching which this text alludes to. This passage is loaded with hidden meaning and requires digging to understand it fully. First, *"I saw you sitting under the fig tree."* Why is that significant? In Jewish minds, the fig tree had become a symbol representing the study of the Word of God. They said the best place to study God's Word was out in nature, in God's world, and that the best place in nature was sitting under your fig tree. Why? Because the fig tree is like the Word of God, it can't be harvested at one picking. Figs ripen in stages, so they have to be picked early every day. Like the Word of God, it can't be understood in one reading, we need to go back again and again.

How did they study the Scriptures? Remember, very few people owned copies of the Scriptures. They had the Scriptures memorized, so they meditated on the word of God.[44] When we mention meditation, we do not mean someone sitting with legs crossed and chanting "Ommmmmmm." These are Hindu symbols for eternity, and this is paganism, spiritualism, and not of God! They didn't empty themselves, as in Eastern Mysticisms. In Hebrew, meditation means to *mutter*, to say something softly to yourself. They had the Scriptures committed to memory, so they could bring a certain passage back to mind, and meditate on it. They filled themselves with the Word of God, saying it softly to themselves, searching its meaning for their lives, thus studying the Scriptures in their minds.

So, if Nathanael was sitting "under the fig tree," obviously what was Nathanael doing? <u>Meditating on</u>

---

44. Bivin, David, *New Light on the Difficult Words of Jesus*, pp. 6-7.

the word of God. By knowing the custom and teaching that underlie this text, we can begin to understand it better. Now, here comes the tough part, the *remez*. Jesus said, "*Behold an Israelite in whom there is no guile,*" or *deceit*. Why would He say that? Jesus was telling Nathanael what he was thinking about. Ok, from that statement, who was an Israelite that was full of deceit?

By William Hallmark ©

The story of Jacob! His name means *supplanter*, one who replaces another. He was deceitful, he tricked his father and his brother. What Jesus was saying to Nathanael was, 'You have been meditating on the Story of Jacob.' That's why Nathanael was taken back. When he hears, "*Behold an Israelite in whom there is no guile,*" he must have been thinking, 'Wait a minute! How does He know what I have been meditating on?' Jesus goes on to tell Nathanael that he knew he had been sitting under a fig tree before Philip called him,' in other words, meditating. Nathanael knew only Messiah could know that.

Jesus showed Nathanael that He is truly the Messiah! He proved, without a shadow of a doubt, who He was, but in a Jewish way! He demonstrated the power of God that the Spirit of the LORD was upon Him. Then Jesus goes on to reveal what scripture Nathanael was meditating on, by his next statement. In John 1:51, He said, "*...you shall see heaven open and the angels of God ascending and descending upon the Son of Man.*" He was referring to Genesis 28:10-17, Jacob's ladder! Jesus is proclaiming 'I am the Gate to heaven, I am the living Tabernacle and you will hear the voice of God, and you will see the power of God being manifested upon Earth.'

Now, what did Jacob see? He saw a 'stairway;' the word ladder is poorly translated. It is a stairway leading from heaven to Earth with Angels ascending and descending, which represents an open heaven. What does Jacob call this place? He said, "*This is truly the House of God, Bethel...This is none other than the gate to Heaven.*" Jesus was saying, "I am the gate to heaven." You see, He didn't need to state that He was the Messiah. With *remez*, He made it clear to Nathanael who He was. He demonstrated the power of God and showed him the Truth! Isn't that awesome! I love this revelation!

What was meant by 'Angels ascending and descending?' The power of the Word of God coming to Earth and going back to God. God's messengers, carrying His Word forth. Jacob heard the voice of God coming from the stairwell. God established a covenant with Jacob, as He had with his father and grandfather. Later, He gave him a new name, "*Israel.*" Israel means,

"One who struggles or wrestles with God." It could also mean, "One who rules alongside God." It wasn't easy for Jacob, but out of that came the whole understanding of Israel and the people called the Children of Israel. Jacob's life, the one in whom was much guile, was transformed by God and was used for God's purposes.

Nathanael loved the LORD and was blown away by what Jesus revealed to him in these few statements. He followed Jesus the rest of his life. This is one example of how *remez* was used to declare His Messianic role.

JESUS IN NAZARETH

The next example that I want to share is found in Luke 4:16-30. Jesus had been in Capernaum, teaching and performing miracles. He went to the Synagogue in His hometown on the Sabbath. He stood up to read and the attendant handed Him the Scroll of Isaiah. Remember, the scripture was not divided into chapters, or verses. He turns to what we call Isaiah 61. He read, *"The Spirit of the LORD is upon Me because He has anointed Me,"* and He continues reading all the different signs of the Messianic Kingdom. He hands the Scroll back to the attendant and sits down. He sat down? I once assumed that He returned to His seat. Understanding their customs explains a lot in this situation. Unlike today, the teacher would sit in Moses' Seat and explain the text or teach a particular subject that he had been studying for years. Archeologists have uncovered stone seats that were engraved, *Seat of Moses*.[45] That's why in Matthew 23:2,3, Jesus said, *"the scribes and Pharisees sit in Moses' seat...whatever they tell you to observe, then observe and do."*

Jesus sat down and said *"Today this Scripture is fulfilled in your hearing."* In verse 22, *"So all bore witness to Him, and marveled at the gracious words ...And said, 'Is this not Joseph's son?'"* In verse 28,29, *"So all the synagogue...were filled with wrath...that they might throw Him over the cliff."* Do you see something wrong here with the way the translators have written this text? <u>They marveled at His gracious words, then they wanted to kill Him</u>. Here is a place we need to stop and dig. This is really very simple, if we know Hebrew. In Hebrew, there are some words that have two meanings that are the exact opposite. 'Gracious' can also be translated, 'disgraceful.' The translators chose to use the word with the positive connotation. So, if we put in the negative word, "disgraceful," it makes much more sense, "marveled at the disgraceful words!"

The question is, why were they so upset with Him when He said the Scripture was fulfilled? Let's look at this, what does the word Messiah mean? It means the *Anointed One.* He said, *"The Spirit of the* LORD *has anointed Me."* Jesus was using *Remez,* and proclaimed Himself the Messiah in a Jewish way and they knew exactly what He was saying! He then uses Elijah as an example of how they were rejecting Him. He reminds them that God's Word came to Israel and they didn't accept it, but someone from another nation did. They were furious with Jesus' words and wanted to kill Him. They took Him to the cliff to throw Him off; this form of

---

45. Flusser, David, *Jesus*, pp. 70-71.

execution was called 'stoning.' There were two ways of stoning, throw the stones on the person or throw the person on the stones. The result was the same, but the latter was considered more compassionate.

Note: at the end of the passage in Isaiah 61, it proclaims, "*the favorable year of the* LORD." The word *favor* equated with the word *salvation,* it means the time of God's salvation. Jesus was saying, "I have come to proclaim God's salvation." Then He stops! The next line says, "*...and the day of vengeance of our God.*" He was not ready to declare the Day of Judgment, because Jesus knew He was coming back to finish the job. He was there to proclaim the first part, to proclaim Himself Messiah, in a Jewish way.

JOHN'S EXPECTATION

Another example of *remez* is found in Matthew 11, the account of the Disciples of John coming to Jesus while he was teaching. John was in prison and he sent his Disciples to ask Jesus, "*Are you the Coming One, or should we look for another?*" John had been preaching that when the Messiah came, He was going to bring judgment, with the winnowing fork in His hand, separating the good and the evil, coming with the fire of God! In Matthew 3:7, John spoke to the Pharisees and Sadducees that came to hear him and said, "*Brood of vipers! Who warned you to flee from the wrath to come?*" He went on to tell them that Messiah was coming with judgment!

What was the winnowing fork? In Jesus' time,

they would harvest the wheat by hand, and beat off the heads onto the threshing floor. The oxen or people would tread it down to separate the husk from the kernel of wheat. They would then take a winnowing fork or fan and throw the grain up in the air, the wind blew the lightweight husk away and the good kernels fell to the ground. When it was relatively clean, they would put the seed between the millstones and grind it into flour in order to make bread. The bad husk would then be destroyed by fire.

Understand, it was not that John disbelieved Jesus, John felt that Jesus wasn't doing the job right! Jesus came preaching peace, love, forgiveness, and relationships, the opposite of John's teachings. So, his question was "are you the one or should we be looking for another?" John knew that if Jesus wasn't the conquering King, he had to get out of prison to proclaim the way for the Coming One.

How does Jesus respond? Matthew 11:4 says, "*Go and tell John what you see and hear.*" He alludes to all of the different references about the Coming One in the Prophets. He uses *remez*, the illusive implication/hint. He goes on to say in verse 5, "*The blind see and the lame walk; the lepers are cleansed and the deaf hear; the dead are raised up and the poor have the gospel preached to them. And blessed is he who is not offended by Me.*" He doesn't have to say I am the King Messiah, He used *remez* and He answered them. John understood what Jesus was saying and was content with His answer.

SON OF MAN

Another example of remez is the term that Jesus used over and over to refer to Himself, '*Son of Man.*' Some think the term refers to His humanity, but it is absolutely the opposite. Adam was called a son of God. We are called sons and daughters of God. Those who believe and accept are to be called the children of God. We are the offspring of God in the Spirit.

Adam, created by God, is called a son of God, in Luke 3:38. But 'Son of God' was used as a unique title for the Messiah and Jesus in a divine sense as well. *Son of Man* does not refer to Jesus' humanity. Son of Man is a *remez*. Look at Daniel 7:13-14, in the vision of Daniel, "*one like the Son of Man coming with the cloud of heaven,*" then He is presenting to the "*Ancient of Days.*" I love that name for God, Ancient of Days. By the way, this passage is in Aramaic. We have very few Aramaic passages, and Daniel has the majority of them. Remember, Daniel lived in Babylon from the time of his youth, where Aramaic had its origin.

There was a different term in Hebrew for son of man, which is not a proper name. We use it as a proper name, and there is nothing wrong with that. But *ben á dam* means, a human being. If you read The *Chronicles of Narnia,* by C. S. Lewis, we find the terms, Son of Adam and Daughter of Eve, that's what it means. In Aramaic it is a proper name, but *Bar Enosh* means Son of Man. When *Bar Enosh* is used, it takes on peculiar characteristics, it's not just any human being![46] This is the word that's mentioned in Daniel. In English, the

---

46. Moseley, Dr. Ron, *Yeshua*, p. 170.

translation of *Bar Enosh and ben a dam* seems to be the same, thus causing confusion. When we see it in the original languages, it is obvious that there is a distinction between the Hebrew and the Aramaic.

When it mentions *Bar Enosh*, it's talking about the Daniel 7 passage, "*...and behold...coming with the clouds...*" Why is this phrase so important? This is an extremely important phrase! What does Jesus say in Matthew 24? How will the Son of Man come? In the clouds! Why is He saying, "*In the clouds?*" He is making a point, He is referring to Daniel 7:13,14; "*He came to the Ancient of Days...is given dominion and glory...that all peoples, nations, and languages should serve Him. His dominion is everlasting.*" Does that sound like a normal human being? He is like a son of man, but He is more than man. He has the qualities of eternity and also the qualities of humanity. See why Jesus used that term? It was the perfect term for Him.

The concept 'Son of Man' was developed more extensively in the Book of Enoch, and very widely known by the people of Jesus' time. He was using *remez* to refer back to Daniel 7. He was not talking about His humanity; He was talking about being like a man, an eternal being who would return in the clouds. He then will rule as King forever, having bestowed upon Him all glory, honor, dominion, and power.[47]

Jesus never said, "I am the Son of Man." He always spoke in the third person. He always said, "*The Son of Man has come...,*" but everyone knew that He was talking about Himself. Every time He used *Bar Enosh*, He was sending a message, He was making a

---

47. Flusser, David, *Jesus*, p. 129.

declaration in their understanding, of who He was, the Messiah!

Why are the clouds so important? Jesus said in Matthew 24:30, *"...the Son of Man coming on the clouds of heaven with power and great glory."* What happened when He ascended into heaven? He disappeared into what? The clouds! In Acts 1:9, what does the Angel say to those that are standing there looking up into the heavens as Jesus goes up? *"This same Jesus who was taken up from you into heaven, will so come in like manner..."* What does that mean? "This same Jesus will return in the clouds." Whoa! He is coming back to finish the job, what the Jews are seeking, <u>peace on earth</u>.

In Daniel 7, the Son of Man will return in the clouds to receive His Kingdom. Why would he say that *"everything must be fulfilled that was written about Me in the Law of Moses, the Prophets, and the Psalms,"* in Luke 24:44? 'The Messiah must first be humbled and then He will be exalted. Then to Him, all authority will be given.' What does Paul say in 1st Thessalonians 4:16,17, *"For the LORD will descend from Heaven with a shout...shall be caught up...in the cloud to meet the LORD...;"* the clouds represent heaven. God will come in power and authority, in a Spiritual way. In 1st Corinthians 15:24-27, Paul speaks of Jesus' authority. In verse 27, *"He has put all things under His feet."* In other words, He is given the Kingdom which is eternal, He earned the right by humbling Himself.

When we read our scriptures, we have a tendency to skip over the list of names, but they are there for a reason. 1st Chronicles gives a list of all the different lineages, and in 3:24, we find the listing of the descendants of David. This is very important. Look closely, what is the last name listed? *Anani,* do you know what *Anani* means? It means *cloud*, in other words, "The Cloud Man!" When the Scriptures were translated from Hebrew into Aramaic, for the Aramaic speaker, it is called the *Targum*, and the translators were called the *Targumim*; just as Hebrew was translated into Greek, for the Greek speaker. When the *Targum* translators came to the passage in 1st Chronicles 3:24, they added a statement in the *Targum*. They said, "...and the final descendent of David shall be *Anani*, which means King Messiah who comes from the clouds." When they did that, it effected the way the Amplified Bible, or The Message, was translated. Is the Amplified Bible, or the Message, a literal translation? No, it is a paraphrase with explanation. The *Targum* translators did not translate literally, they often paraphrased, and put in comments to make it more understandable.

Why would they say the last descendent of David will be King Messiah? Because *Anani* means, the Cloud Man! This translator did not want the reader to miss that point. So, why King Messiah? Because He is the Man that comes in the clouds, based on Daniel 7. That's why all the references of coming in the clouds, in the New Testament, are important. They were confirmations in the Jewish minds of His identity, of the Truth! The truth that He is the King with the everlasting Kingdom; the one that all authority is given to; the One they have been looking for!

So what did Jesus say in Matthew 28:18? *"All authority in heaven and on earth has been given to Me."* Why? Because He has been exalted after the crucifixion, after the resurrection, He is now exalted! He is now King of Kings and LORD of Lords, Name above all names, established on His throne, sitting at the right hand of the

Father. He is the King who will come in the clouds!

The King comes in two ways. The first King's coming, in Zachariah 9:9, says, *"Rejoice greatly, O daughters of Zion! Shout, O daughters of Jerusalem. Behold, your King is coming to you. He is just and having salvation, lowly and riding on a donkey, a colt, the foal of a donkey."* The second coming of the King, "He shall come with the clouds." The First Century Jews did not understand that the same King was going to come twice. Do you see where they would get the idea that there were two Messiahs? The important thing here is to realize that the same Messiah is coming back "in the clouds" to finish His work! This is why the Resurrection is vital to the understanding of how Jesus could return. We proclaim, on Resurrection morning, He is alive! He is, and He will return to finish His work, "even so, come LORD Jesus!"

CHAPTER SEVEN
WHAT CHANGED

MESSIANIC CLAIM BECAME BOLDER

One of the jobs of the Sanhedrin was to observe teachers to see if they might be the Coming One, the Messiah. Since the Messiah could not proclaim who He was, they were to be the ones to judge. They even sent observers out to see if John the Baptizer was possibly the Coming One, Matthew 4:12. With Jesus, they sent out observers and later began testing Him, but something changed. The High Priest and some of his close associates began to look for a way to discredit Jesus. Why? Jesus became a threat to their positions with the Roman government. Originally, the High Priest had been a very godly leader, who sought God's will for the nation and the people. He came to that position through the inherited bloodline of Zadok. Antiochus Epiphanes sold the High Priest position to Jason. [48] When the nation came under the rule of the Romans, the position of High Priest became a purchased position. In other words, the High Priest was appointed by Herod and he sold it to the highest bidder. Israel was the only captured nation that was allowed to continue with their forms of worship: temple worship, sacrifices, and Priestly leadership; however, to say the least, it was a volatile time. That was why the High Priest would rather keep everything running smoothly than for the Messiah to be revealed. Jesus threatened their livelihood. The more the people accepted Jesus as their Messiah, the greater the

---

48. *4 Maccabees* 1:15-20.

danger became that things would turn violent, and the Jews would try to overthrow the Roman rule.

One example of their attitude changing toward Jesus, is found in John, chapter 7. John tells us in 7:37-39 that Jesus stood during the water libation at the Feast of Tabernacles, *Sukkot*, and cried out: *"If anyone thirst, let him come to Me and drink. He who believes in Me, as the Scripture said, out of his heart will flow rivers of living water."* John goes on to explain in verse 39 that Jesus was speaking of the Holy Spirit. When the people heard Jesus say this, they thought back to the Scriptures of Isaiah and Jeremiah. They knew the Word, they knew their Scriptures, and they knew what Jesus was saying. In Isaiah 12:3, it says, *"Therefore you will draw water from the well of salvation."* What is Jesus' name in Hebrew? "<u>Yeshua</u>," which translates to <u>Salvation</u>. In Jeremiah 2:13, *"For My people have committed two evils, they have forsaken Me, the fountain of living water..."* and Jeremiah 17:13, *"Oh LORD, the hope of Israel, all who forsake You shall be ashamed. Those who depart from Me shall be written in the earth, because they have forsaken the LORD, The fountain of living water."* In John 7:40, the people say, *"Truly this is <u>The Prophet</u>!"* In other words, surely this is the Messiah!

The Feast of Tabernacles, *Sukkot*, was considered the great in-gathering, the <u>season of pure joy</u>. It not only celebrated God's provision of the harvest, but it was also a reminder of God's provisions during their 40 years in the wilderness, and their expectations of the coming of the Messiah. With Messiah's coming, there would be peace and dwelling in the presence of God forever and ever. On the last day of this great celebration, called *Hoshana-Rabbah* or the Great Hosanna, the last of the 70 sacrifices for the 70 nations, representing all Gentiles, were brought into the Temple. They would sing Psalm 118, and wave palm branches as the priest poured out the water libation. It was a reminder that God had brought about Salvation, He was going to set up His Kingdom, and send His Messiah. Verse 26 says "*Blessed is he who comes in the name of the LORD!*"[49] Psalm 118 was also sung at the conclusion of the Passover meal.

Things were getting heated so the Sanhedrin sends out a group, but this time it was not to test Jesus, but to try to trap Him. In John 8:1-12, they bring a woman who had been caught in adultery, and ask Jesus, what should be done to her. *"Jesus stooped down and wrote on the ground with His finger."* He said, *"He who is without sin among you, let him cast the first stone,"* then he bent down and wrote in the dirt again. We know that no one is without sin, no matter how righteous, everyone has sinned, except for Jesus! So they left, beginning with the oldest. Now, look back at what had just happened at the Feast of Tabernacles. Tie the statement Jesus made about the fountain of living water to Jeremiah 17:13. God said, you have abandoned Me, the fountain of living water, and "*those who depart from Me shall be written in the earth.*" You can't tell me that these learned men weren't going to that Scripture in their minds. I can imagine they were thinking, 'is he writing my name, does he know about my sins?' Jesus was using *remez* in the form of prophetic gesturing here.[50] They gave up that time, but they kept trying to trap Jesus with His own words.

---

49. Howard, Kevin and Rosenthal, Marvin, *The Feast of the Lord*, pp. 141-142.
50. *Jeremiah* 27:1-18, *Acts* 21:11, examples of Prophetic Gesturing.

THE TRIUMPHANT ENTRY

By William Hallmark ©

The last straw for the High Priest was when Jesus entered Jerusalem riding on a donkey, the people welcomed Him shouting 'Hosanna,' and singing portions of Psalm 118, *"Blessed is He who comes in the name of the LORD!"* Mark 11:8, tells us that they laid palm branches and their *"clothes on the road."* Do you realize what "clothes" they were laying on the road for the donkey to walk on? It was their outer garment, the <u>garment with fringes</u> on the four corners that represented their righteousness and the Law. Also, waving the palm branches represented not only welcoming royalty, as in a king; it also represented victory, rejoicing, and eternal blessings. This is full of meaning. They were, in a very Jewish way, proclaiming <u>Jesus, King Messiah!</u>

They knew their scriptures, they knew Zachariah 9:9-11, that said King Messiah would come humbly, riding on the colt of a donkey, with righteousness and salvation. We would expect the King to come in riding a white horse, in majesty with a great army behind Him. Jesus came just the way they expected Him to. They did expect the conquering King, but not conquering His enemies with great warfare. He would rule with a <u>peace that will never end</u>! He would establish Jerusalem as His capital and a united Israel as His nation. He would drive out His enemies and make peace with all nations.

The people saw Him as fulfilling the prophesies exactly. The way they welcomed Jesus represented the last day of the Feast of *Sukkot*. All of the other feasts will be fulfilled, except the feast of Tabernacles, *Sukkot*. It represents dwelling in His presence, the feast that will never end. The very things they did to welcome Jesus proved that they knew that the Messiah had come. His fame had already spread because of the miracles, but especially because of the miraculous raising of *Lazar*. It tells us in John 12, the crowd that followed Him was there when *Lazar* was raised from the tomb. The people knew that this was one of the major Messianic signs, they <u>believed He was the Messiah</u>.

The Pharisees knew what the people were saying by their words and their actions. In Luke 19:39, they say, *"Teacher, rebuke Your disciples."* They were getting very nervous, it seemed everything was culminating, and they were scared of Rome. Jesus was coming from Jericho, and that road led straight into the Temple proper, through the <u>Eastern Gate</u>. I believe Jesus went straight in and cleansed the temple.

OVERTURNING THE TABLES

Jesus went to the Temple and cleans House. Let's look at this closely. The account is in all four Gospels, but I am going to quote from Mark 11:15-17: *"Is it not written, My house shall be called a house of prayer for all nations? But you have made it a den of thieves."* Did Jesus lose His cool? Did His temper get the best of Him? It sure looks like it did, but remember, if Jesus was acting out of His own anger, He had just sinned. One sin, just one sin disqualified Jesus as the sacrifice for the sins of the world. Remember the Law, Leviticus 6:6, tells us that the sacrifice for trespass sin must be without blemish. One blemish, one spot eliminated that ram from being an acceptable offering. Only one sin would have disqualified Jesus from being the acceptable sacrifice. Remember what Jesus said, *"He can do only what He sees His Father doing,"* John 5:19.

So what was going on here? First, let's look at Isaiah 56:6,7; it says, *"the sons of the foreigners who join themselves to the L<small>ORD</small>...for My house shall be called a house of prayer for all nations."* Jeremiah 7:11, *"Has this house which you call by My name, become a den of thieves in your eyes? Behold, I, even I have seen it, says the L<small>ORD</small>."* Jesus was connecting the scriptures in Isaiah and Jeremiah, stringing pearls. He was quoting God's words, and making it His own. What was happening? They were selling and exchanging money in the court of the Gentiles. The non-Jewish believers came to the Temple to pray to God, and there was all this stuff going on. It would be like someone setting up a yard sale in the middle of your sanctuary during morning worship. Yes, Jesus was angry because God was angry. These people were stealing God's praise. There were all sorts of booths for selling offerings and areas to exchange money before going on the Temple Mount proper, and there was no reason for them to set up in the court of the Gentiles. Also, again Jesus was using Prophetic gesturing, for in forty years, every stone of that great Temple would be torn down. This really angered the Jewish leaders, and they began to plot how to kill Jesus, Mark 11:18. This was the final straw as far as the High Priest and his followers were concerned.

WHO KILLED JESUS

Now, I want to move to a topic that is very important to me. Who killed Jesus? The reason this topic is so important is because the historical Church has done a great disservice to the Jewish people down through the ages. The church has proclaimed for centuries that the "Jews killed Jesus!" I've heard Jewish people say that, even as children, the first time they heard the name of Jesus or Christ was when someone called them, Christ killer!" We are talking in America, in our generation! During the middle ages, Monks in black robes paraded around synagogues that they had set fire to, carrying crosses and singing, *Christ we adore You*, while people inside were burning to death. They did this because they saw every Jew as a 'Christ killer' and felt that they deserved what they got.[51] That is a lie from the pit of Hell!!

---

51. www.wikipedia.com, Persecution of the Jews.

Who really killed Jesus? We are going to be detectives, digging deep for the meaning of the Scripture. We want to read to find what the Scripture is really saying, to dig for the truth. So, with understanding, let's look at the text with care.

At the trial and crucifixion of Jesus, how many of you have heard that the people who welcomed Him on Palm Sunday were the same people that cried out "crucify Him?" I've heard preachers preach that, and I even preached that at one time myself, and there is nothing further from the truth. If we dig deep, we will see why this is not true.

The first question we need to look at is, <u>what was the betrayal of Judas</u>? Most people say, "He gave Him a kiss." This is how Judas identified Him, because it was dark. Another common answer given is, "He betrayed their relationship." Judas did much more than that. He had just finished breaking bread with Jesus, in Jewish understanding that was entering into covenant![52] Most people miss the true betrayal, why? Because this is a very emotional subject and so often the answers people give are emotional ones. I believe Judas was not doing this maliciously! I believe he thought he was doing the right thing in getting Jesus before the Sanhedrin, in order for Him to be heard.

In all likelihood, Judas was a Zealot. I believe he thought that if Jesus went before the Sanhedrin, they would declare, "Jesus is the Messiah!" He went to the Sanhedrin because Jesus wouldn't go on His own, so <u>he forces the issue</u>. Do you see the lie of the enemy? I believe his whole point was, "Let's get it over with, so

---

52. Stern, David H., *Jewish New Testament Commentary*, pp. 227-228.

we can overthrow the Romans. We can get our country back and Jesus will be our King!" Most likely, Judas thought that when Jesus was declared Messiah, the people would rise up in rebellion! As a matter of fact, the worst crime a Zealot could commit was to turn a fellow Jew over to the enemy. When he recognized that the High Priest had tricked him, that they wanted to turn Jesus over to the Romans all along, he couldn't live with the guilt, so he killed himself. If it was Judas' plan to betray Jesus, he certainly would not have killed himself! He was duped by the enemy into thinking he was doing the right thing.

Let us look at the question again: What was the betrayal of Judas? He showed them where Jesus was. That's the whole point, he showed them, but under what condition? <u>This is the key</u>. What was the condition? The Sanhedrin knew where they could find Jesus; He went to the Temple every day. They could have arrested Him anytime they wanted. In Matthew 21:46, it tells us, *"they sought to lay hands on Him but feared the multitude."* They could have arrested Jesus except for their <u>fear of the people</u>! The people loved Jesus. They knew He was the Messiah, the King that had come to save them; they were ready to proclaim Him King! *"Hosanna to the Son of David! Blessed is He who comes in the name of the LORD! Hosanna in the highest,"* Matthew 21:9b. These are Messianic claims. Palms represented the independence of Israel. Palms became a symbol for independence under the Maccabees.[53] Why did those welcoming Jesus into Jerusalem use palm branches? It was a way of saying, "Our King has come! We're going to be free!

---

53. *1 Maccabees* 13:49-52.

We're going to have our own nation back!" This is dynamic in its high drama, the entry into Jerusalem, the high Messianic expectations. They also believed that Messiah would make His appearance at Passover. Everything was meeting their expectations. How did Jesus enter Jerusalem? Riding on the colt of a donkey. When they saw that, they thought of Zachariah 9:9, *"Your King comes to you with salvation, lowly and riding on a donkey, a colt, the foal of a donkey."* That means deliverance! They truly believed He was the One.

During the week of preparation for Passover, Jesus' teachings ignited the High Priest and his henchmen. They were desperate to arrest Jesus before His teachings incited the people, and caused the hand of Rome to come down on them. They convinced Judas to show them where He could be found *"in the absence of the multitude,"* Luke 22:6. Jesus and his disciples were finishing Passover, as well as everyone else in Jerusalem. Jesus and his inner circle, the eleven disciples, went to the Garden of Gethsemane, an Olive grove, to spend the night.

Archeologists have found a cave in the Garden, and also the remains of two olive presses. More than likely, Jesus' Disciples were sleeping in this cave. Why? This was the time of year when there was dew and it could get quite chilly at night. In Luke 22:55, it tells us that they kindled a fire in the courtyard to warm themselves. In Mark 14:51,52, it says that one of His Disciples was wearing nothing but a tunic when the soldiers grabbed him, he ran off into the night naked. It makes sense that the disciples would have slept in the cave. We also know that Jesus did not sleep, but prayed in the garden all night. It says that Jesus went out from them; so scholars now believe that 'went out' refers to 'out of the mouth of the cave.' They agree that this was probably where they were staying. Judas knew where the garden was and that they often stayed there. This was not the time of the olive harvest, so the presses were not being used, so it was a perfect place to go in and sleep. Have you ever wondered why Jesus didn't return to Bethany (Mark 11) after the Passover, as He had done all that week? Jesus followed the law perfectly. Passover was considered a High Holy Day, so the rules for *Shabbat* were to be followed. The Garden of Gethsemane was within the allotted distance from the city walls for a Sabbath's Days journey, approximately 2,000 cubits.[54]

The Temple soldiers go in and arrest Jesus. There is a question as to whether they violated Jewish Law. The Law said that they could not hold a capital offense trial without waiting two days and allowing the defendant to call witnesses. They did not do that, they did everything in one night; most likely with the inner council of twenty-three, it took at least twenty-three of the seventy Sanhedrin members to make a quorum.

<u>The people didn't even know that Jesus had been arrested until He was on His way to the cross.</u> Why else would the women be crying? Why was it that when the men walked by and they looked at the cross, they beat their breasts? That was a sign of mourning and sadness. This was the Man that they thought was going to lead them to victory, their King, their Messiah, and He was dying! They were grieving. These people were not the ones that cried, "Crucify Him!" His arrest was done in

---

54. Hayford, Jack (General Editor), Nelson's New King James, *Acts* 1:12.

secret, they had His trial during the night, and He was in Roman hands before the people even woke up that morning. Passover went late into the night and the daylight hours of that day were a holiday. It was the first full day of the Feast of Unleavened Bread. It was a feast day, a High Sabbath, so the people were not going to be opening up their shops or working in their fields, or doing any regular work, so the people were not out in the streets early.

The Sanhedrin had His trial, He was sent to Pilate, then to Herod, then back to Pilate, and sentenced to be crucified after being beaten. He was on His way to the cross before the people realized what has happening, and they wept and mourned. This whole thing was done in secret. That is the whole point, not even the whole Sanhedrin was notified. The High Priest, more than likely only notified those that agreed with him. If Nicodemus, Joseph of Arimathea, and others had been there, they would have tried to stop them.

So, who was it that said, "Crucify Him?" Some will say that it was the Pharisees and the Sadducees. The leaders! I can say positively that it was not the Pharisees, and here is how we know: When Pilate brings Jesus out and said, *"Behold, your King!"* What do the people cry? Remember, we're reading like detectives. <u>*"We have no King but Caesar!"*</u> Now, which of these groups would make a declaration like that? Sadducees or Pharisees? There was no way that the Pharisees would say that! One-Hundred times a day they would pray, *"Baruch atah Adonai Elohenu, melech ha-olam,"* *"Blessed are You, O LORD our God, King of the Universe."* Who is the King? <u>God is King</u>! A Pharisee would rather die than to say that they have no King but Caesar! They were always getting into trouble because they would not bow down to Caesar. The Pharisees believe that God is King. The Kingdom of God was one of their themes. They would never say, "We have no King but Caesar."

So who makes up the crowd? The High Priest and his henchmen. Now, understand, there were over 3,000 employees in the Temple. The Temple guards were under the employment of the High Priest and the Priesthood. They were the ones that arrested Jesus, so when they brought Jesus out, <u>the High Priest and the Temple guards cried out, "Crucify Him! Crucify Jesus!"</u>

It was the plan of the High Priest, because Jesus threatened the Temple. They trumped up charges against Him of blasphemy but they couldn't put anyone to death, so they had the Romans do it for them. They made all sorts of charges against Him in front of Pilate, and finally, because Rome was always worried that there would be a revolt, they carried out the sentence. At Passover, a feverish pitch would arise because of Messianic expectations. Herod would actually come in from his palace and stay in Jerusalem during Passover week, in case there was trouble, and extra guards were brought in to help keep things calm. Knowing this was going to be happening, the High Priest felt they had to get rid of Jesus before things got out of hand.

Now, what did the Sadducees cry out when Pilate washed his hands? Pilate said, *"I am innocent of the blood of this Man."* They responded, *"Let His blood be on us and on our children,"* Matthew 27:24,25. The Sadducees were the Temple officials, and the curse they spoke came true! Forty years later, what happened to the Temple? Their Temple was destroyed, they were killed or scattered, and their children had lost their heritage of being Priests in the Temple of God! The curse, the blood, came upon them and their children, exactly as they had spoken it. What you speak comes back on you, measure for measure!

So who killed Jesus? If we are talking about the responsible parties, they were the High Priesthood and the Sadducees in connection with the Romans, because the Romans carried it out; so, <u>calling Jews, "Christ Killers" is a lie</u>! There was only a small segment of the Jews involved for political, economic, and social reasons. It is often political, economic, and social pressures that cause us to choose the wrong way, not God's way!

The Sadducees were the dominant group in the Sanhedrin, and they would have been the inner council. The High Priest would have had his twenty-three select members that agreed with him present to pronounce the death sentence. More than likely, there wasn't a Pharisee among them. If so, it would have been a very corrupt Pharisee, but even a corrupt Pharisee would not have been able to make the statement, "We have no other King but Caesar."

If you want to talk about guilt though, I have to add a few other things to be considered. No one killed Jesus. He said in John 10:18, "<u>*I lay down my life. No one takes it from me*</u>," so let's realize that is the truth. If people would realize that, they wouldn't be persecuting Jews over Jesus' death. So, we have the Sadducees and the Romans. Jesus laid down His life and God did it! Jesus was *slain from the foundation of the earth*, Romans 13:8. It was God's will that this would happen. Jesus had to die for the sins of the nation, and for the sins of the world; God used the corruption of people, but it was still God's plan.

Here is the preaching aspect of it, you and I did it! It was our sins that nailed Him to the cross, He died for us, and so we are all guilty in that sense, because if it had not been for our sins, He would not have had to die. Physically and historically, it was the High Priest, his henchmen, the Romans, and some of the Sadducee leadership. They're the ones who saw to it that Jesus was put to death.

TWO MESSIAHS

The crowd saw Jesus as the coming Messiah, but they also saw Him as the conquering King, the Son of David. They believed that there would be two Messiahs. Why? It was inconceivable that the same Man could come twice. It was not physically possible. They knew that there was going to be a Messiah, the suffering servant. The concept of two Messiahs had developed into a common belief. The first one was Messiah, son of Joseph. I find it amusing that Jesus' earthly father was Joseph. They also believed that there was going to be a conquering King, Messiah, son of David. Anytime you see the name David or "Son of David," or "My servant David," this is the conquering King image. God said in Ezekiel 37:24, *"I will make my servant David, King over them."* David had been dead a long time, by Ezekiel's time. What was Ezekiel talking about? He was proclaiming King Messiah; David was a code word for 'Messiah.'

That's why, when the blind men in Matthew 9:27

cried out, *"Son of David, have mercy on us,"* the Disciples tried to shut them up! Why? If the Romans heard, they would arrest them because they knew this Messianic claim of a conquering King. The blind men kept getting louder, Jesus came over and said, *"What do you want?"* They answered, *"Heal us Jesus,"* and Jesus healed them.

Many in Israel had decided, 'obviously we have suffered, so we must be the suffering servants.' By the time Jesus had come, they were looking for the conquering King. They do not realize that He was going to be both. Their understanding was too methodic. How could they understand two comings of the same person? That's why Isaiah 53 said, *"Who has believed our report?"* He goes on to say, *"He was cut off."* This was a Jewish way of saying 'to die prematurely, before he was old.' In fact, Daniel 9:26 says, *"the Messiah shall be cut off, but not for Himself,"* not because of what He has done, but for the sake of others. Isaiah said, *"He will be cut off...they made His grave with the wicked, but with the rich at His death."* This is the perfect description of the events of crucifixion. It goes on to say, *"He shall see His seed,"* His offspring. They couldn't understand how He could die young and yet live to see his offspring. That's why Isaiah said, *"Who has believed our report?"*

There are teachings, even today, that the nation itself fulfills Isaiah 53, because they had suffered so much. We are told in Leviticus 6:6 that the sin offering was a pure innocent lamb without spot or blemish. The sin offering took the place of the one who had sinned. If it was Israel's iniquities (sins) that they paid for, then they would have died, the nation or the Jewish people would no longer exist. God set up the sacrificial system so Israel would not have to die. According to God's plan, how could Israel be the one *"afflicted for our iniquities"* when Israel was the one committing the iniquities? They were not sinless, they were blemished, thus they could not have been the acceptable offering.

We have all sinned and fallen short of the glory of God. Romans 6:23 tells us, *"The wages of sin is death."* It is clear that God chose to have One to pay for the iniquities of Israel and all people. Jesus was that lamb without spot or blemish that paid the price for us all. Jesus was sinless, that is why he could die for our transgressions.

In the Jewish Synagogues today, they read from the *Torah* each week. *Torah* is the five Books of Moses. They also read the *Haftarah*, which means *after the Torah*. They read through the Scriptures in one year, beginning at the Feast of Tabernacles. They begin that day reading and rejoicing in the Law. My understanding is that when they read from the Prophets, they will read Isaiah 52, then skip to 54! Hmmm, I wonder why? It's because their parishioners ask too many questions about Isaiah 53. More Jewish people have come to the LORD after reading Isaiah 53 than by any other passage in Scripture. They realize Israel never died, the nation was scattered, but they never died. The ones that have come to a belief in their Messiah realize that Isaiah 53 is talking about a Person, Yeshua (Jesus)!

The concept of two Messiahs points to the first and second coming of Jesus. His first coming was as the suffering servant that took on the sins of the world. Do you see why the resurrection is so very important? Through the resurrection, it was made possible for Jesus to return. How will He return? Back to Daniel 7; He will return in the clouds as the conquering King!

ON THE THIRD DAY

Now, let's go to the question of the death of Jesus. When did the resurrection take place? <u>On the third day</u>! Here are some quotes from Jesus' words: Luke 24:7, "*The Son of Man must be delivered into the hands of sinful men, and be crucified, and on the third day rise again.*" Mark 10:34, "<u>And on the third day He will rise again</u>." Matthew 27:64, "*Therefore command the tomb be made secure until the third day...*" In Luke 24:21, as the two followers of Jesus traveled to Emmaus, they stated "<u>today is the third day</u>." So, what does the quote from Matthew 12: 39,40 mean? "*It will be as it was in the sign of Jonah, as Jonah was three days and three nights in the belly of the great fish, so will the Son of Man be...in the heart of the earth.*" Jesus was saying, '<u>I will be really dead</u>!' Many have taken that one verse and discarded all the others. Not realizing the First Century Jewish understanding of time, it sounds like Jesus was saying He had to be in the grave for three days and three nights. Yet, other Gospels say, <u>on the third day</u>. If it had been three complete 24 hour periods, resurrection would have been <u>on the fourth day</u>, not the third day.

The Jewish understanding of time is different from ours. Their day ends when two stars are visible, at approximately 6:00 pm, and the next day begins. They take their reasoning for this from creation. In Genesis 1:5, "*God called the light Day, and the darkness He called Night. So the evening and the morning were the first day.*" God began the first day in the evening and continued it throughout creation, so it made sense to them to copy God's pattern. They divided their day into two 12 hour periods. We see this in John 11:9, Jesus replies, "*Are there*

12 hours in a day." The first 12 hours began at sunrise, so their ninth hour would be our 3-4 pm.[55] With this understanding in hand, we know Jesus was taken down from the cross at approximately 3:00 pm. How do we know that? Matthew 27:46, also Mark and Luke said it was about *"the ninth hour,"* and Mark 15:42 says, *"Now when evening had come, because it was the Preparation Day, that is, the day before the Sabbath."* Luke 23:54 says, Joseph of Arimathea took Jesus' body, for it was *"the day of Preparation and the Sabbath drew near."* The Jewish Sabbath begins at sunset on Friday and ends at sunset on Saturday. John 19:31 tells us, *"Therefore, because it was the Preparation Day, that the bodies should not remain on the cross on the Sabbath…the Jews asked Pilate that their legs be broken."* You see, it could take up to 36 hours to die from crucifixion; it was a slow and horrid death.

In the Jewish understanding of time in the First Century, if there was at least one hour left before sunset, it counted as a full day! From the time of Jesus' death, they had at least an hour on Friday, all day Saturday, and more than likely ten hours of Sunday. In their way of counting time, that would make His Resurrection on the third day.

What about the three nights? Three days and three nights were symbolic for totally dead, completely dead, in other words, it was not a natural resuscitation. Jesus' point in Matthew 12:40, *"three days and three nights,"* was, 'I'm going to be really dead, just like Jonah!' Now, why is that important? It states in the Apostles Creed, "He descended into Hell…." This was not talking about *Torment*. The concept came from the

---

55. www.agapebiblestudy.com, Jewish Time Division.

Greek understanding of Hades, which was where all the dead would go, the good and the bad. *Sheol* was divided By William Hallmark into the place for the good and the place for the evil, as in the story of Lazarus and the rich man, Luke 16:25.

By William Hallmark ©

What is the point of that statement, 'three days and three nights?' He really died; He went where dead people go. The accusation was that Jesus didn't really die. The modern, supposed scholars have written documents about how Jesus didn't really die, He revived, and His Disciples hid Him. He lived a long life and married Mary Magdalene and they had children. Similar thinking still exists. An example would be the book, *The DaVinci Code*. Look at Matthew 28:11, we see how old this lie really is. It tells us that the soldiers were bribed to lie. I ask you, how many people would die for a lie?

Most of Jesus' disciples were martyred: crucified

(Peter upside down), thrust through, boiled in oil, stoned, and skinned alive.[56] Who would die for a lie, much less such horrible deaths? People will always believe what they want so that they can do what they desire to do without guilt.

The point of Jesus' statement *"three days and three nights,"* was very specific, 'I was really dead.' This was a **miraculous resurrection**! A change took place in His body. It was a new body, He could walk through walls, He could appear and disappear, He could eat, and He could be touched. He said to Thomas. *"Stick your hand in My side."* He looked like Himself, in that He was recognized by His disciples and over 500 witnesses, yet He was different.[57]

---

56. www.ichthus.info/ Disciples/intro.html
57. Hayford, Jack (General Editor), Nelson's New King James, 2nd *Corinthians* 15:6.

RESOURCES

JOHN'S RECOMMENDATIONS

We have barely scratched the surface of all of the treasures there are in the Word of God to be revealed. Hopefully, this has piqued your interest and given you a zeal to understand scripture more completely. Here are some resources to help you begin your own adventure of discovering the wonders of His Word! *There is a bibliography on pages 128,129 that John handed out to his students. Below are his comments about some of the recommendations.

I want to list some materials that I recommend for your use as resources. Obviously, we use the Bible as our main source. Jesus quoted scripture all the time, and His scripture is what we call the Old Testament. These are suggestions of books that will be helpful in your studies. Starting with the New Testament translation and commentary, which I have found to be of great value in my studies.

I highly recommend David Stern's, *The Jewish New Testament & Commentary.* He takes the New Testament and puts it back into many of the Jewish understandings. When he uses Hebrew words, he has a list of definitions in the corner of the page, which makes it an easy read. It is an excellent study tool. In the Commentary, he goes into the background and it is very informative. I consider *both* a very valuable resource. He has also translated *The Complete Jewish Bible*. David is a Messianic Jew who lives in Israel.

The writings of Dr. David Flusser, a Jewish

Orthodox Rabbi and a teacher at Hebrew University, are very good. He and Dr. Robert L. Lindsey, a Baptist missionary to Jerusalem and Pastor of the Narkis Street Baptist Church, collaborated and were really the fathers of the contemporary 'Jewish Roots' movement. They made many discoveries that turned modern scholarship upside down. Dr. David Flusser wrote several books, *Jesus,* and *Jewish Sources in Early Christianity,* to name a few. He taught about *Yeshua* (Jesus) on Israeli Armed Forces Radio for the Secretary of the Army.

Alfred Edersheim was of Jewish heritage and became a Cleric in the Anglican Church. He was a great and prolific writer. I can't say that I agree with every one of his conclusions, but he had some of the most complete and best resourced books you can find on Jewish culture. He was an avid scholar and he read the Talmud and the Jewish writings. He wrote, *The Life and Times of Jesus the Messiah, The Temple,* and *Sketches of Jewish Social Life.* I also recommend *Jewish People of the First Century* by Shmuel Safrai.

When people ask me, what is the best book to start their Jewish Roots studies with, the one I recommend is *Yeshua,* by Dr. Ron Moseley. At the end of each chapter, there are questions that can be used as a study guide, or for teaching a class. It goes into misconceptions concerning the Law, Jewish idioms in the teachings of Jesus, Jewish background in the early Church, the Pharisees and their teachings, their rise to power, and their influence on the early Church. It's an easy read, and it really gives a lot of information to start with, that really whets the appetite.

Others writers are Brad Young, ORU Professor of the Old Testament. He has written several books: *Jesus,*

The Jewish Theologian; *The Parables*; *Paul, The Jewish Theologian*; and *Jewish Background of the LORD's Prayer*. These books are much more scholarly books.

David Bivin wrote, *Understanding The Difficult Words of Jesus;* it centers on the theme of the language that Jesus spoke. There is an appendix that explains background and Hebrew context. His newest book is, *New Light on the Difficult Words of Jesus*. It centers around more of the life and teaches of Jesus, and there is a glossary of terms that is very helpful.

David Bivin lives in Jerusalem and is the former president of the Jerusalem School of Synoptic Research. The school is a consortium that Dr. Lindsey and Dr. Flusser put together, it is made up of scholars who believe Scripture and are searching the New Testament for the hidden truths. These scholars are from all over the world that are part of this. Alva Rhine, David Bivin, Dwight A. Pryor, Brad Young, Marvin Wilson, and Dr. Bill Bean, to name a few. They get together periodically to study, discuss, debate, argue, and enjoy the zeal of discovery. Their desire is to understand and uncover what the original text is saying. There are also Jewish scholars in the group, because they learn more about the Second Temple Period from Yeshua (Jesus) than from any other Rabbi!

Marvin R. Wilson's *Father Abraham*; *Listening to the Language of the Bible* by Lois Tverberg and Bruce Okkema; and Bill Bean's *New Treasures,* are all good books. Leen Ritmeyer is one of the leading archeologists of the Temple Mount. He has written several articles on the Temple Mount, and where the Holy of Holies was. He uses measurements to prove his theory, a fascinating work. He has been written up in the 'Biblical Archeology

Review.' If you read *BAR*, realize it is not a Christian publication. Their archeological discoveries are fascinating.

Another source is, *The Splendor of the Temple* by Alec Garrard. He made a model of the Temple. Wonderful work, and very fascinating!

I do also want to mention the writings of Josephus as a resource, *The Jewish Wars*, and *Antiquities of the Jews*. Paul L. Maier has written an excellent book entitled *Josephus*. Jewish Roots Studies have become more popular, thus there are more books than I can list. These are some I am personally familiar with. They are all very good resources as well.

Everyman's Talmud, by Abraham Cohen, is a summarization of the *Talmud* and it is really a good reference book! It's not really a sit down and read book, but a great research book. The *Talmud* is a compilation of sayings and discussions of the Rabbis from about 50 BC until 200 AD. About 250 years' worth of teachings and discussions, compiled by Judah the Prince. There are two *Talmud*, The Babylonian *Talmud* and the Jerusalem *Talmud*. The Babylonian *Talmud* is much more comprehensive and the one that most people quote. The Talmud itself is made up of two parts The *Mishna*, which is a commentary and reflections of the Rabbis on Scripture and Scriptural principles, and the *Gemara*, which is a commentary on the *Mishna* along with their reflections on the *Mishna*. They are grouped according to Tractates: on the *Mishna*, according to themes, like baptism. *Everyman's Talmud* will give you a good view of the Talmud, and what the Jewish background was. The resources are out there; you just have to be willing to dig!

I can't tell you the number of books that I have researched and the number of historical documents that I've read in order to find the materials that I have put together for the teachings of Christ in the Passover presented in the Seder.[58]

Hidden Treasures Revealed is part one of a two-part book series. Part two will cover Jesus' understanding of salvation, the Kingdom of God / heaven, relationship with the creator, the breaker passage, and the great commandment to name a few. It is my hope to have it ready for printing within a year.

~*Diann Phelps*

---

58. *John's sources came from many years of research and there are some that I am not aware of. However, I have been able to find much of this information on the internet, for the footnotes.* **Statement by Diann Phelps.**

SUGGESTED BIBLIOGRAPHY

BASIC BACKGROUND STUDY

Cohen, Abraham, *Everyman's Talmud*, Schocken Books, NY, 1949, ISBN 0-8052-1032-6.

Edersheim, Alfred, *The Life and Times of Jesus the Messiah*, Word Bible Publishers, Inc. (new updated edition, complete and unabridged in one volume), ISBN 0-529-10085-1.

Edersheim, Alfred, *Sketches of Jewish Social Life*, Hendrickson Publishers, Peabody, MA, ISBN 1-56563-005-X.

Edersheim, Alfred, *The Temple*, William B. Eerdsmans Publishing Co., Grand Rapids, MI, 1994, ISBN 0-8028-8133-5.

Wilson, Marvin R., *Our Father Abraham*, William B. Eerdsmans Publishing Co., Grand Rapids, MI, 1989, ISBN 0-8028-0423-3.

BIBLE STUDY AND COMMENTARY

Stern, David H., *Jewish New Testament Commentary*, Jewish New Testament Publications, Inc., Clarksville, MD, 1992, ISBN 965-359-008-1(Hardback), ISBN 965-359-011-1 (Paperback).

GENERAL STUDY

Bean, E. William, *New Treasures*, Cornerstone Publishing, Minneapolis, MN, 1999, ISBN 0-9623950-2-1.

Bivin, David, and Blizzard, Roy, Jr., *Understanding the Difficult Words of Jesus*, Destiny Image Publishers, Shippensburg, PA,

1994. (*Center for Judaic-Christian Studies*, Dayton, OH)

Moseley, Ron, *Yeshua*, Ebed Publications, Hagerstown, MD, 1996. (*Arkansas Institute of Holy Land Studies*, Sherwood, AR)

Young, Brad H., *Jesus the Jewish Theologian*, Hendrickson Publishers, Peabody, MA, 1995. (*Gospel Research Foundation*, Tulsa, OK)

Young, Brad H., *The Parables*, Hendrickson Publishers, Peabody, MA, 1998. (*Gospel Research Foundation*, Tulsa, OK)

Young, Brad H., *Paul the Jewish Theologian*, Hendrickson Publishers, Peabody, MA, 1999. (*Gospel Research Foundation*, Tulsa, OK)

RESOURCES FOR SELECTED WORKS

Center for Judaic-Christian Studies, P.O. Box 293040, Dayton, OH 45429, www.jcstudies.com

Gospel Research Foundation, Box 703101, Tulsa, OK, 74170, www.gospelresearch.org

Arkansas Institute of Holy Land Studies, 9700 Hwy 107, Sherwood, AR, 72120, www.aihls.org

INDEX OF TERMS

Abraham 4,38,62,63
Adonai (LORD) 66,67,113
Aiyin ra'ah (Evil eye) 51
Aiyin tovah (Good eye) 51
Anani (Cloud Man) 99,100
Aramaic (Semitic language) 12-16, 49,97,98,100
Atonement 5,66
Avi (My Father) 37
Avinu (Our Father) 37
Bar Enosh (Son of Man) 97,98
Ben a dam (Son of Adam) 98
Caesar 113-115
Circumcision 44
Circumlocution 64-69
Dead Sea Scrolls 14,43
Diaspora (dispersed Jews) 18
Disciple (student) 8,12,17,21,26,28,32,38,40,42,44,57,71,85,86,89,95, 106,111,117,121,122
Eli, Eli, lama Sabachthani (Jesus' words from the cross*)* 16
Eliyahu (Elijah) 16
Emperor Hadrian 7
Essenes (Sect of Judaism) 14,43
Excommunicate 28,29
Gethsemane 4,111,112
Green Tree 21,85,86
Haftarah (Scripture after the Torah) 118
HaShem (The Name) 69
Hatag (kill) 81
Hoshana-Rabbah (Last day of *Sukkot* celebration) 103
Idiom 50,51,53,124
Jehovah 66, 67
Josephus 15,126

Kal va-homer (Light and heavy) 77,78
Kosher (Allowed) 6,60,76
Lazar (Lazarus) 32,33,106,121
Mammon (riches) 49
Masoretic Formula (Developed vowels) 67
Meditation 90
Messiah (Christ) xiii,xiv,1,5,7,21-29,33,34,36-42,44,45,58,68,84-87,89, 92,94-97,99-106,109-112,116-118
Messianic (Signs or times of the Messiah) 5,21,23-26, 33, 36,60,66,67, 93,106,110,111,114,117,123
Mikva'ot (Plural of *Mikveh*) 43
Mikveh (Baptismal Pool) 43
Mishnah (Written sayings of the Sages) 14
Mishnaic Hebrew (Hebrew spoken, 550BC-22AD) 14
Moses' seat 93,94
Naaman 29
Nathanael 89-93
Nazarene 30
Ossuary (Bone box) 31
Palestine 7
Parables 70-75,77
Papias 17,18
Passover 34,104,111-114,127
Pharisees (Sect of Judaism) 2,28,33,40,43,57,94,95,106,113-115,124
Prodigal 71,74,75
Prophet/Prophesy 2,3,18,19,24,26 28,53,86,85-89,96,99,103,104,106, 108,118
Question for Question 35,36
Rabbi (Teacher) 14,15,19,22,24,25,29,35-37,43,46,54,59,60,70,77,78,82, 85,86
Rabbi Hillel & Shammai 60,86
Rabbi Jochanan ben Zakkai 86
Rabshakeh 12,13
Raca (Term of slander) 79

Ratzach (murder) 81
Remez (Hint or illusion) 21,39,84,86,88,91-98,104
Royal Portico 34
Sadducees (Sect of Judaism) 40,95,113-115
Samaria/Samaritan 13,14,24,25,29,30
Sanhedrin (Supreme Court) 60,86,102,104,109,110,112,113,115
Seder (Order) 127
Shabbat (Sabbath) 82,112
Shekinah (Glory) 27
Sheol (Place of the dead) 121
Shamayim (Heaven) 48
Shiva (Sitting seven, mourning) 32
Shroud of Turin 30
Sukkot (Feast of Tabernacles) 103,106
Supplanter 91
Synagogue (House of study) 28,29,46,93,94,108,118
Syncretistic 67
Tallit (Prayer shawl) 6
Talmud (Commentary on the Mishnah) 42,72,74,124
Targum (Aramaic translators) 100
Telos (Goal) 53
Tetragrammaton (Four letters) 66
Torah (First 5 books) 46,55,118
Yeshua (Jesus in Hebrew) xiv,1,3,5,8,13,14,30,103,118,124,125,129
YHWH (God's Holy Name) 65-67
Yod & *Kotz* (Jot & Tittle) 55-57
Zacchaeus 38
Zadok (High Priest line) 102
Zealot (Sect of Judaism) 85,86,109,110

www.ingramcontent.com/pod-product-compliance
Lightning Source LLC
Chambersburg PA
CBHW070810100426
42742CB00012B/2321